THE ENEMY OF
KINGS

Cover design by Sara Young
Cover illustration by Stephen Jon Ming
Photography by Stephany Clark

ISBN: 978-1-954089-88-4   1 2 3 4 5 6 7 8 9 10

Printed in the United States of America

THE ENEMY OF
KINGS

Defeating the
World's culture with a
Kingdom lifestyle

LOUIS EVANS

KUDU

CONTENTS

CONTENTS

PROLOGUE

On December 14, 2011, during a devotional journey through the Word, I found myself in the book of Proverbs. In March of the following year, I was drawn to go back to the beginning of this Book of Wisdom, dust off my *Strong's Exhaustive Concordance* and examine the words of the Hebrew to unlock a deeper meaning I knew must be waiting for me. By the beginning of October 2012, I began to hear God speak to me about writing a book. *Wait a minute . . . God; you've got to be kidding!* I never wanted to write a dissertation (which deterred me from pursuing a doctorate), much less a full-blown publication. However, God relented and insisted this would not be like so many books currently lining the shelves of Christian bookstores. This would be a bold (and even dangerous) treatment of how we have been assigned to live as aliens in a hostile world system and walk in radical obedience to the laws of Christ.

Before I get started, let me tell you my story. I was born in 1961 to a Black-American father and a White-British mother. They met while my father was stationed in England with the US Army in post-World War II Great Britain. As my father's tour was coming to a close in 1957, my parents decided to get married and live in the US. The years after military service were tough, and black men in America during those times were the "last hired and the first fired," so work for dad was difficult to find. One of my earliest memories of my father was him mopping a floor at a business, so he would be able to feed us. My three sisters and I were born during the late '50s and early '60s. These were difficult financial times and in the shadow of the escalating Vietnam conflict.

Our lives changed when dad decided in 1966, at thirty years old, to rejoin the military; however, this time it would be the United States Air Force. His old US Army career field (Combat Engineer) had become critically short of manpower in the USAF. This was the beginning of an odyssey of sorts for our family, taking us from my hometown of Highland Falls, NY, to Plattsburg AFB, NY, then on to North Dakota, Southern California, across the Atlantic to England, then back across to Massachusetts, up again to Highland Falls, NY, on to Northern California, and then across the Pacific Ocean to the Western Pacific Island of Guam. Though we moved and traveled often, Dad traveled quite a bit more. From 1966 through 1973, Dad served four one-year tours of duty in Thailand. Though a close-knit nuclear family, we suffered from all the dysfunction caused by an alcoholic, absentee father. Though he quit traveling after 1973, he was unable until much later to relate to me as his son. We were so unlike each other: He was a bear of a man and bigger than life. I was scrawny and insecure. He made his living with his hands. I dreamed of being a scientist. As time passed and I entered middle school and puberty, I began to ask questions: *Who am I? Why am I here? Where am I from? What is my purpose?* These questions begged answers the religious traditions of my parents did not possess. My father's religious background was Missionary Baptist, and what should have been for him a source of strength and power, was instead strewn with a family history of sexual hypocrisy and abuse. My mother was of the tradition of the Church of England which, though quaint, was cold. It was orderly but powerless; it had history but no hope. So, I began to look for my own answers. In 1973, I saw a special television documentary about unexplained mysteries and lost civilizations. It was narrated by Erich Von Daniken, author of *Chariots of the Gods*. The "mysteries" though real were misleading; nevertheless, I devoured the book when I bought it and looked for more. I read everything I could get my hands on about pyramids, UFOs, Atlantis and other ancient civilizations, the Bermuda Triangle, and even, the Bible. As remarkable and unbelievable as some of the biblical accounts are, the Bible was the last place I was willing to look for answers to some of the deep, dark mysteries of the world and universe.

In November 1973, my father was reassigned to Northern California. As it turns out, we moved next door to a biracial family like ours, called the Freemans. I became friends with their sons and would go to their house to hang out quite often. In the process, I became acquainted with their mother, a rather joyful and vocal Pentecostal Christian who ALWAYS talked about Jesus. I thought she was rather peculiar but was fascinated by the stories she would tell about Jesus, the miracles He performed, and His imminent return. I was hungry for the supernatural, so even though I was young, I loved to converse with her about miracles and end-time prophecy. One day, she asked me if I had ever, "Asked Jesus into my heart?" I told her that I hadn't, and asked her how. She said, "Ask Jesus to forgive your sins, and come into your heart, to be your Lord and Savior." After continuing to hear her scary stories about the Last Days (and not wanting to be "left behind"), I decided to give my life to Christ, so in February 1974, while lying on my bed, staring at a crack in the upper right-hand corner of my ceiling, I asked Jesus to forgive my sins and come into my heart. I didn't use any religious jargon (I didn't know any!) or fancy religious language, I just spoke to him like He was in the corner of my ceiling.

This was, without a doubt, the most important event of my life! It has affected everything else in my personal history. My oldest sister thought I had lost my twelve-year-old mind! It was okay and even desirable for me to be religious and go to church and read my Bible—as long as I kept it "in church." However, I was not (at least in her mind) allowed to make it part of my daily life. This faith in Christ became my compass in life and my map to lead me in the way to go. It preserved me and protected me and brought me liberty from bondage.

With "unsaved" parents and no spiritual guidance, I started to attend the chapel on base and then the youth meetings on Sunday evening. My growth was steady, and with Boy Scout events and time with my new friends, I was able to guard my life and stay out of trouble. However, as I began to make the transition to high school, my life began to change again. High school basketball, sports events, and dances began to take the place of Boy Scouts and friends. Life began to revolve around the typical adolescent male subjects: girls and sports. My life in Christ continued to move forward albeit painfully slow, and I found myself desiring acceptance from my peers and attention from girls more than the approval of God. I was enjoying my high school years (probably more than I should have been) and was unprepared for what came next.

At the end of my sophomore year in high school, I discovered to my absolute horror, that my father was being reassigned to the island of Guam in the Western Pacific! I was finally achieving a level of respect and popularity among my peers and even positive attention from the girls I knew. I would be moving in the middle of my junior year of high school. What a disaster—or so I thought! However, God was moving even when I could not see it, and late in the summer of 1977, I was able to attend a Bible conference taught by a popular national Christian youth teacher. This was the first real Bible training I had ever had. I immediately took two things away from this seminar: 1) To repent to my father of my rebellion and put myself back under his authority, and 2) Form the habit of daily Scripture reading.

Upon arrival on the island, we were immediately put up in a fancy tourist resort. The only problem was the resort catered almost exclusively to Japanese tourists. There was a TV but only ONE local channel, and most of the tourists at the hotel spoke no English. That wasn't even the worst of it. When we were able to move into our new house, and I started school, I was devastated by the school I had to attend. It had the architecture and feel of a prison block, and I did not want to be there! But knowing I didn't have a choice in the matter, I just went. I no longer cared about my grades; I just wanted to get through. The only consolation at the time was that I was a 6'4" basketball player, and the coach was excited that he would be able to make me a part of his team. Nevertheless, even in our disappointment and uncertainty, God never abandons us or leaves us to our own devices. Even when *we* forget, God doesn't!

Shortly after moving into our new base house, I was invited by one of the neighborhood kids to a youth meeting at his church. When I arrived at the meeting, I was stunned by the size of the group. My old youth group had about a handful of kids. This one had about two dozen, and they were serious about their faith in Christ. Later, I was to find this was fairly common on the island at that time. In April 1978, the month I turned seventeen years old, I began a relationship that was destined to change the course of my life. During this time, the church youth group was invited to a pool party sponsored by another youth group. It was there that I met someone with whom I would develop one of the most important relationships of my young life.

Before I continue, I need to discuss an issue of my life that I struggled with during this time. At the age of six years old, I was introduced to pornography by an older kid in the neighborhood where I lived. It started out with looking at

Playboy magazines in the woods and progressed to reading hard-core pornography by the time I was in middle/high school. It was something I struggled with until I left home. Having someone to discuss my problems with was instrumental in eventually overcoming them. During this period in my life, my father was distant and not available for much of anything—especially not a discussion about my problems. The worse part of this period was dealing with the shame that would wash over me like a wave. It felt like it would engulf me. If this is something you've experienced, don't lose hope. God does not abandon us when we struggle!

As I was saying, I met a guy during the summer of 1978 who I called Willie. He was a year younger than me at the time. (I was seventeen. He was sixteen.) One day, he was at my house, and I asked him to disciple me. Amazingly, he said, "Yes." Now, this guy was no joke! He taught me to read my Bible and hear God's voice. He taught me to pray, and he taught me how to share my faith and lead people to Christ. This is someone who led a schoolteacher to Christ when he was fourteen, and God used him to change the course of my life! I learned an important lesson about God as well. He can use anyone He wants to get just about anything done in your live that needs to be done. I was so desperate for God to move in my life, I pursued someone younger than me for help. The lesson here is that you shouldn't allow the package your help comes in to prevent you from receiving it.

The next three years after this were spent growing in Christ and being a testimony to my parents who both gave their lives to Jesus during the summer of 1980. The time God chose to capture their lives, was ironically, during a period when my heart was far away from Him. The next lesson I learned here was not to ever think that God's faithfulness is dependent on us. God can deliver His Word through the mouth of a donkey if He deems it necessary. It was another humbling lesson for me. Though my father was saved now, it would still take a few years of God working to heal our splintered relationship. Even though my dad made rapid progress those first few years, the foundation of our relationship was shaky from years of neglect and required time to rebuild damaged trust, and the open wounds of past rejections needed to heal. If these are issues you have struggled with, know that they must be dealt with, or they will continue to create problems in your life long after your "childhood" has ended.

By December 1 of 1981, I had decided to join the military myself and was on my way to USAF Basic Military Training, aka boot camp. It was a wonderful time of learning and (ironically) freedom! God blessed me with numerous opportunities to share my faith with the guys I trained with, and for the first time in my life I began to have opportunities to learn leadership skills that would have been a challenge in a home environment devoid of a father's presence. By June 1982, I was transferred to Carswell AFB outside of Fort Worth, Texas. Shortly after arriving on base, I met some believers and started attending Grace Temple in Fort Worth where, in August of 1982, I was baptized in the Holy Ghost. This ushered me into a new period of spiritual life: a clear awareness of the presence of spirit beings—both holy and unholy. The anointing I received made me a clear threat to the kingdom of darkness, and the enemy attempted to overwhelm me during this time, but because I knew my authority in Christ, I was able to stand my ground.

In spite of the teaching I received, I did not guard my emotions and entered into an unwise relationship in November 1983, and in October of the following year, I was married. It was a bad decision for both of us as we both had past unresolved family dysfunction. The lack of a father presence in our childhoods had devastating consequences upon our reaching adulthood, and in February 1999, after fourteen excruciating years, our marriage ended. In July 2000, the courts gave me custody of our four children, ages (at the time) sixteen, thirteen, twelve, and ten.

The period immediately following this was one of great joy and liberation; however, it was also a time of great emotional stress and difficulty. I discovered I was a wonderful father but a lousy mother, a good provider but an inadequate nursemaid. It was a period of learning to truly lean on God and to draw my strength, wisdom, and understanding from Him. I rediscovered how to pray and hear God's voice. One night while praying, the presence of God was so strong in the room, I opened my eyes and turned around, fully expecting the Lord God to be standing there behind me. This was a period of rapid growth. The Word of God was alive! Every book I read and every sermon I heard was living!

In 2002, after almost twenty-one years of service, I left the Air Force and sought employment in the private sector. With a BS and two AS degrees, I felt confident I would be able to find new employment very quickly. With almost three months of vacation time accumulated, I was certain I would have enough time to find work before my military pay ceased. However, it was not meant to be. I had to sell some jewelry to buy groceries before I realized I had to do anything I could to pay the bills and feed my children. So I did some work demolishing a building and then started delivering pizza for a local chain. I did this until the beginning of June 2003 when I started working for a defense contractor in the area.

This period of unemployment was the time God elected to use to bring my future wife into my life. While looking for a job, I drove a couple of miles every day to the local town library where I used one of the computers to go online and job hunt. I submitted resume after resume, hoping and praying for a "hit." After weeks of this process, in order to relieve the mind-numbing boredom, I started visiting a Christian website that brought me in touch with a woman from the Netherlands. I thought it was "safe" and she wouldn't come knocking on my door the next day, so we became "email buddies" (kind of like pen pals, except through email). From the end of July through October 2002, we wrote to each other about our children, our families, church life, the Word of God, prayer, and our hopes and dreams. We never exchanged photographs or talked on the phone. We were just simply buddies becoming best friends until one day I thought to myself, *Louis, you tell this woman everything in your life. What is going on?* It was at this point that I had realized the emotional attachment that had developed between us. I was falling in love with a woman who amazingly enough I had never seen even a picture of! *What does she look like?* I asked myself, *Is she homely? Is she attractive?* Then I realized . . . I really didn't care. She was the woman I had always dreamed about, and she loved my God with all her heart!

The next year and a half were a blizzard of activity. I flew to the Netherlands to meet her children and church (and get the approval of her pastor). She came to the US with her two children to meet my girls and church family. Then I went back to Holland again to meet my future mother and father-in-law, and finally, on July 31, 2004, we were married in the US—in Macon, Georgia. At the writing of this book, I'm still in love, and she is still the woman of my dreams!

So, why am I telling my story? We all have a unique story because we are all individuals. However, in the United States and Canada, an epidemic of fatherlessness has created a great leadership void, especially in our young men. What God desires to do in us will never reach fruition without a father's wisdom. Though my father and I ultimately had a wonderful relationship as adults, the void that was created in my life as a boy took years to repair and in turn created voids in my relationships with some of my children that created pain and have taken much time to continue repairing as well. The principles set forth in this book will provide detailed instructions on how to live and walk in God's wisdom and authority and navigate the world we live in. This is a book every father should read, learn from, and live. Then, when he has absorbed it, he can teach it to his boys. Only then can the sons of the King exert dominion over the enemy of kings.

PARADISE LOST

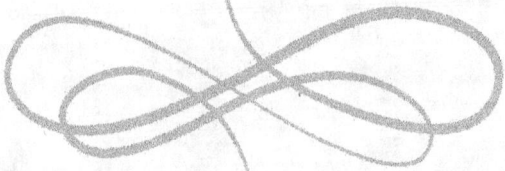

CHAPTER 1

IN THE BEGINNING

When I was a preteen, I loved to read comic books. In fact, I had a substantial collection. I had Superman, Spider-Man, Iron Man, Wonder Woman, Luke Cage, and even Iron Fist (the first three issues!) among others. I would read them every chance I got. My earliest memory of a comic book hero was a 1965 issue of Iron Man shooting energy balls out of his hands and chest, flying through the air and saving the world from evil. I often used to wonder what it would be like to possess superhuman abilities, to fly through the air like Superman. I would dream about flying through outer space and exploring the stars with the Green Lantern. It wasn't just their physical attributes . . . their special capabilities . . . and their superhuman powers; it was their strength of character and willingness to sacrifice everything for the good of all men.

During my childhood, I attended Sunday school and heard the stories of the Bible. They were often told by sweet ladies with good intentions; however, they were terribly uninspiring. The male characters like King David and Jesus were not portrayed as the manly men that they were but ordinary and boring. I understand they were teaching elementary-aged boys, but they failed to reveal the power and dynamism of the men they taught, great men of power and authority that inspired the imagination. Without someone to look up to and aspire to, all I figured I could do was stick to my comic books.

> Without someone to look up to and aspire to, all I figured I could do was stick to my comic books.

After reading about one of these superheroes, I'd look into the clear summer night sky and ask myself, *How did the universe get here, and how was it made? Who am I? Why am I here, and what is my purpose?* Some of us asked these questions as children, others as adults.

> *In the beginning God created the heavens and the*
> *earth, and the earth was without form and void and*
> *the Spirit hovered over the face of the deep.*
> —Genesis 1:1

In *The Divine Romance*, Gene Edwards recounts how in eternity past, the eternal God was the "Self-Existent One," who existed alone before anything else was created. In all the vastness of time and space, He was all there was, until the moment He saw in His mind, a people . . . a bride . . . someone to share His heart, mind, and purpose with.

The plans of the all-knowing God led to the creation of a new and totally unique life-form; a spirit being that lived in a physical body. In order to create this new species, *Elohim* had to create a physical realm; an environment in which this being would not just survive but live and thrive. Prior to this, the Creator had only made a spiritual, metaphysical realm for Himself and servants with names such as angels, archangels, cherubim, and seraphim. This realm was called heaven. These were purely spiritual beings, exclusively made for the purpose of fulfilling the requirements of the living God in His spiritual kingdom. Following *Elohim's* creation of the spirit world, He spoke into existence a physical one. After creating time and space, He formed and made the sun, the moon, the stars, and other celestial bodies, as an expression to His people of His creative power and a demonstration of His awesome might. When you consider the immense beauty and utter perfection of the heavens, you are tempted to wonder whether or not God wasted time and space on something we only look at in the night sky. However, everything was created intentionally for God's own purpose. At this point in the creative process, the earth was a barren mass of rock, yet God's Spirit hovered over it in anticipation of what was coming next. The earth was indeed uniquely created for a specific purpose at the center of the heavens!

And God said, "Let the earth bring forth grass."
—GENESIS 1:11

The first thing God called forth from the dry and water-covered ground was unconscious plant life. It is here we learn two things about God: 1) He never starts anything until He finishes it, and 2) Spoken words matters.

God planned everything before He spoke, and He understood as our Creator two very critical issues. First, with a need for oxygen, God brought forth from the ground first a producer of oxygen for all the creatures, as well as a consumer of respiratory waste—carbon dioxide. By the third day, the light of the sun provided the plant life with the means for photosynthesis. This complex process provided the plants with the energy required to bring forth food from the earth and a means for the nutrients and minerals of the earth, necessary for proper human functioning, to be consumed by the human body to support it. God created all plant life with seed, with the ability to reproduce itself, because nothing grows without seed.

> And God said, "Let the waters bring forth abundantly the
> moving creature that hath life and fowl that fly above the
> earth in the firmament of heaven. . . . Let the earth bring forth
> the living creature after his kind, cattle and creeping thing,
> and beast of the earth after his kind;" and it was so.
> —Genesis 1:9

The second life-form the supreme God called forth were the creatures of the water and the air. Again, the Creator spoke and commanded, "Waters, swarm with living creatures, and let creatures also come forth and fly above the revolving face of the earth under the lofty protective arc of the atmosphere known as the firmament."

The third time God spoke, He called forth from the earth the land creatures both great and small. These living, breathing creatures were "conscious life." The supreme God commanded the ground to produce living creatures, and they came out of the ground alive and fully functioning, according to their species. Some were very large, and others crept on the ground. It's interesting to note the word "beast" above is the Hebrew word behemoth. This is the same word used in Job 40:15-24, to describe the giant beast that walked upon the earth, described in v. 17, as a creature that "moveth his tail like a cedar." This describes the Apatosaurus and the other great creatures that walked upon the earth during his time.

The order of creation was very specific, and very intentional. It reveals the perfect order of the supreme God with everything in its proper time.

1) Earth was made to include dry land, the seas, and the firmament. These non-living materials were used to build the structure of the earth, used to house and protect all created life.

2) The plants were to be food for the earth's inhabitants as well as an oxygen generator. Their environment is the dry land and to a lesser degree the seas.

3) The fish and myriad sea creatures were at home in their aquatic environment, called forth from the waters.

4) The birds of the air had their habitation in the lower atmosphere; they too were called forth from the waters.

5) The animals were called forth out of the dry ground, depending on the land to support them.

And God said, "Let Us make man in our image, after our likeness; and let
them have dominion over the fish of the sea and over the fowl of the air,
and over the cattle, and over all the earth, and over every creeping thing
that creepeth upon the earth." So, God created man in His own image,
in the image of God created He him; male and female created He them.

—Genesis 1:26

Elohim's final ultimate, declaration was actually to Himself. That THEY would bring forth a creation called man; a species that would be a physical representative image of the Eternal God on the earth. This new race of beings, though created, would be immortal and as *Elohim's* representatives, would have His power and authority; Psalms 93:1 says, "He is clothed with majesty, the Lord is clothed with strength," and what is true of God would be true of them. Moreover, because they were created in His likeness, they looked like Him as well. It was God's desire that they subjugate, rule over, and crush down every creature in every environment. This I believe would have especially applied to Lucifer and the forces of darkness as I believe one of the earliest purposes of these regents would have been to judge and punish these rebellious ones. Crushing down and subjugation of the earth would be part of that. Battling the forces of darkness would be their destiny, to protect the creation from them, and I believe keep them from infiltrating any part of the earthly environment.

Therefore, God created the first man and woman as His own representatives, and in doing so He created the species in two equal but different halves, man and woman. They, He declared, would subjugate the earth and everything in it together! That is why the creation was very good! Because it was perfect for the assignment it was created for.

> *And God blessed them and said, "Be fruitful and multiply and*
> *replenish the earth, and subdue it: and have dominion."*
> —GENESIS 1:28

Elohim gave the couple a congratulatory blessing, and then charged them to bring forth fruit. I can almost hear the voice of the supreme God say, "If you are my representative image, I want what is from me to grow out of you." God desired for His character, wealth, power, and authority to be manifested in and through them! He continued, "And then I want your power and authority to be multiplied by your ability to procreate until the earth is overflowing with copies of yourself!" They were to do this by depending on their source of life, which was God Himself! Just as the fish were called out of the water and could not live without it, it was for God's representative whom He called out of Himself. This was significant, because up until this point nothing had the power to multiply; as angels had no counterpart, they were unable to multiply themselves. In the process God desired for humanity to subdue the earth and its inhabitants, to conquer and bring it under subjection and rule it with perfect justice. *Elohim's* desire was that they dominate the earth and rule it together as coregents—as king and queen.

Though the heavenly beings God created first were powerful and glorious creatures, it is they who were assigned to serve men. Man, not angels were created in God's image, and given God's representative authority over the earth and everything in it. This included the angels that were cast down to earth and placed under man's dominion.

And the LORD God formed man of the dust of the ground, and breathed
into his nostrils the breath of life; and man became a living soul.
—GENESIS 2:7

So important and vital was man to the original plan and purpose of God that, the way the self-existent One created them is considered a mystery. You see, every other creature was "called forth" from the earth or the waters. However, to form man, God the master sculptor, used clay earth, and formed by His own hands an exquisite sculpture of His own likeness. How magnificent it was! Every bone, every sinew, every muscle, every organ, down to the finest the most irreducibly complex cellular structure in the man's body was formed. Then He did something amazing. He breathed into the inanimate clay figure, and the creative process was completed. He literally breathed spirit life into the man! God created the man's spirit and then breathed it into the physical body He formed! Adam's eyes opened, and he began to move and breathe on his own. He was an individual, a moral free-agent, but he was completely dependent on God as his source!

The tree of life also [was] in the midst of the garden,
and the tree of knowledge of good and evil.
—GENESIS 2:9

The tree of the knowledge of good and evil could not have existed if evil did not already exist on the earth. Not only did God have to give man an opportunity to obey or disobey Him, He also had to give mankind the opportunity to accept the assignment that He had for them. The choice was stark and laid before them absolute clarity.

Mankind's choices were:

» Be a royal (king/queen) under the authority of the self-existent God, and dependent upon Him; along with the assignment of protecting the earth and judging Lucifer.

» Be a slave of Lucifer, and independent from God.

If man chose to accept the assignment, he would be the instrument of God's judgment to crush down and subjugate the forces of darkness. By creating man in His image, God made him just one level below Himself (Psalms 8:5). In reality the difference between mankind and God was that God has no beginning and no end. Mankind, on the other hand, was created a race of immortal beings. This desire for immortality has never left man because he was never meant to die.

Partaking of the tree of life was the means of accepting the assignment, and with the assignment came eternal life on earth. So, then as now, man's destiny was and is a choice! Once they chose eternal life, which was again dependent on the King of kings, they would be able to accept the assignment to destroy, crush down, and subjugate the forces of darkness on the earth.

> *And the LORD God took the man and put him into*
> *the garden of Eden to dress it and keep it.*
> —GENESIS 2:15

God placed Adam in a magnificent garden east of the land of Eden. The word *Eden* in the ancient language means "pleasure and delight." The name speaks of an environment of great beauty and sensuality. There was no need for houses because the environment was perfect: no hot sun, no cold rain, no wind, no danger. The environment was perfect! For the same reason, there was no need for clothing. They ate from the trees, plants, and vines, and they must have experienced a great deal of physical intimacy! This was a place fitting for a king and queen to live voluptuously. This garden would be the incubator to unleash the explosive growth of the new royal family until they had taken over the whole earth.

God's purpose in His sensual design was to encourage the couple to be sexually intimate with great frequency:

» To increasingly cement their unity of soul.

» To give them pleasure and joy in one another's bodies.

» To procreate, multiply, and fill the earth with copies of themselves.

» To create a model revealing God's heart of passionate love towards them.

Adam's assignment was to take care of the planting, tilling, and watering of the garden; it was easy, pleasurable work. He was also charged with guarding, protecting, and surrounding it to keep the enemy out. The enemy, in this case, was Lucifer and the other rebellious angels.

And the LORD God said, "It is not good that the man should be alone;
I will make him an help meet for him. . . ." And the LORD God caused a
deep sleep to fall upon Adam, and he slept; and he took one of his ribs
and closed up the flesh instead thereof; and the rib, which the LORD God
had taken from man, made he a woman, and brought her unto the man.
—GENESIS 2:18-22

Again God declared, "It is not best for the man to be solitary. I will prepare and bring forth a counterpart, whose assignment it will be to aid and protect the man." In verse 21, "alone" can also mean "separate" or "apart." It's almost as if God were saying, "It's not good for those two to be apart," so God opened Adam's body, removed a bone to harvest DNA, and built a woman for the man from scratch. Why God did it this way is a mystery, until you gaze across the future millennia to a bloody Roman crucifix. When the Man's body had fallen limp, an unknown Roman soldier thrust his spear into the Man's side, out of which sprang forth blood and water, redemption and life, His life, both of which were necessary to bring forth His own bride.

The supreme God then anesthetized the man, bringing him to a death-like state of consciousness. He was probably clinically dead until the Creator brought him back to life. He then took one of his ribs, to use to build the woman, forming a bond that was impossible to truly break. After removing the rib, God closed up and repaired the tissue underneath, so there was not even a scar. Then God completed His desire to create them "male and female." The woman was in the man the whole time. The man's "Love of his Dreams" was then taken by God and led to him.

The word God used to describe the woman, "help-meet" is the Hebrew word *ezer*. This is derived from the Hebrew verb *azar* meaning, to "surround" that is protect or aid. Most men consider their wives as helpers maybe, but protectors? It was at this juncture of primordial history that woman's original assignment was announced. Just as Adam's assignment was to surround and protect the garden, it was the woman's job to surround and protect the man!

These were their assignments:

» The man's job was to till the garden and protect it from Lucifer and the other fallen angels. He was fully equipped with authority and dominion, and because he represented God upon the earth, his power was exercised through his mouth. With Lucifer's heavenly power stripped from his fall, Lucifer would have no choice but to back down and flee at the voice of the king.

» The woman's job was to rule and dominate with the man; however, her most important job was to guard and protect him.

And Adam said, "This is now bone of my bones, and flesh of my flesh:
she shall be called woman, because she was taken out of man."

—GENESIS 2:23

When Adam first saw the woman, he must have been pretty excited! I can see him bragging to all the animals, pointing to her saying, "This is MY woman!" I can almost hear him boast, "This woman—she shares my bones and she has a body like mine. Only beautifully different! She will be proudly and loudly called woman because she was drawn forth out of me." It was here that God ordained the sexual relationship between men and women. God decided that for all time. It was the man's responsibility to leave his mother and father's household in order to pursue his queen. Sexuality was never meant to exist except in a sumptuous, royal environment. The man was to chase after and become united with his woman. This was an environment where shame and disappointment did not exist.

Adam was so incredibly passionate about his woman! Whereas God formed him from clay and breathed life into him, the woman was built from Adam's body. Adam's DNA came directly from God, and the woman came directly from Adam. God's desire from the beginning was to create mankind as man and woman. The way God chose to accomplish His purposes is a mystery. God chose to form this royal couple in a similar manner as another couple in an age yet to come. You see, when this bride was formed, she came out of the side of her betrothed the "last Adam" while he slept. How can this happen? Before the need for redemption arose. Could it be that it happened a second time because God's divine order required it?

How thou art fallen from heaven, O Lucifer, son of the morning!
—Isaiah 14:12

When Lucifer led the rebellion against *Elohim*, and a third of the angels were deceived and followed him, Lucifer was ejected from God's presence and sent to the earth with the other rebellious angels. The self-existent God could have imprisoned the instigator of this rebellion on any one of the planets, moons, or asteroids. So why send him to the planet at the center of His purpose and passion?

In God's desire for a counterpart, He desired one like Him, so He created a people, a species, a royal family, a divine representative that had His power, authority, and majesty. Thus, in the eternal mind of God, before He said, "Let there be" anything, there existed one who was like Him, whom He could love and be loved by in return, freely and under no compulsion. He desired this royal bride; one who would think like Him and have His heart, desire, and character. However, the whole enterprise was fraught with risk.

In the Psalms 8, King David asked the philosophical question of the ages, "What is man. . . ?" We all understand man as a complex interaction of organs, chemistry, thoughts, and emotion, but what is his purpose? The Hebrew phrase is a pure interrogative that could also be translated "why man?" or even "what good is man?" That frail mortal whom God marked out for remembrance. This son of Adam, who because of the rebellious choices of his forefathers, lives in a sinful, corrupt fallen world. God has marked man for remembrance and cares for him. So then, what is the eternal purpose of man? As sons of Adam, their original purpose was to rule the earth. The dominion mandate was to strengthen them until they were no longer immature children but mature, responsible adults able to enter into their inheritance.

But that's not how it turned out. Instead of doing what they were destined to do, the first man and woman chose instead to listen to the wrong voice, and thus pursue their own way. Because Adam failed his assignment to protect the garden, Lucifer was allowed entrance to the place that they would call their home. The serpent, as we know, was the most intelligent and subtle of all the creatures in the garden, and because he had not yet been cursed, he was probably the most beautiful creature as well. It's possible that he could have walked on two legs like a biped but at the same time move with great grace and elegance.

Now I want to stop here and take a moment to explain something. Oftentimes, Eve is blamed for the failure and rebellion of the first couple; however, because it was Eve's assignment to protect the man, the serpent determined that he must deceive HER and set out to do so. If the serpent had attempted to deceive the man, Eve would have known to intervene. Instead, the serpent deceived Eve, and the man for whatever reason chose to intentionally disobey God. Lucifer went after the woman because she was the man's protector! The enemy knew that it was humanity's assignment to march out onto the field of conflict to enforce God's purpose. You see, it was not Eve who was the weak link in this case, but Adam!

The result of this choice, to eat of the tree of the knowledge of good and evil, acted to transform obedience to rebellion, dependence to distrust, and intimacy to enmity. Whereas the royal couple first walked in obedience desiring to do their Father's will, now they desired to do their own will. Where they once walked in dependence, relying on their Maker for everything, now had to work for everything in sweat and labor to provide for their own needs. At one time, Adam walked with God in the cool of the evening, while the evening breezes caused the trees to gently sway; Adam enjoyed the company of the most high God. Unfortunately, for Adam that was no longer possible because he had discarded that relationship in favor of something else he valued more. This is the ultimate cause of every problem and every dysfunction mankind has ever faced because without obedience, dependence (submission), and intimacy with God, man's desire to serve himself will end up destroying him.

In the beginning, even though man physically walked with God, faith was still necessary for dominion—not faith that God was, but faith that He could be trusted. The fall was not just a deception of the woman. It was lack of faith on the man's part. True faith will always be manifested in a rock-solid dependence on Him!

AFTER THE FALL

And the eyes of them both were opened, and they knew that
they were naked; and they sewed fig leaves together, and
made themselves aprons. . . . Unto Adam and to his wife did
the LORD God make coats of skins, and clothed them.
—GENESIS 3:7 AND 21

Following the rebellion of man, the two former regents hid from God. It was time for their walk with God "in the cool of the day," yet they could not be found. Their Maker repeatedly called for them. "Adam, Adam, Where are you?" The glorious God never asks a question He doesn't already have the answer to. When they finally answered, the man said, "I heard your voice and hid because I was naked." When they came out from behind the foliage, God was heartbroken at their feeble and panicked attempt to cover themselves. They were no longer clothed with His glory. Instead, they were pale and terrified, trying to use their hands to cover areas where the fig leaves they had haphazardly assembled were tearing, exposing their nakedness, which now caused shame even though they were alone! In God's compassion and great sadness, He killed innocent animals, taking their hides to cover the shame of the man and woman. These were very first sacrifices for sin. The very first blood ever shed was to cover the shame of the first man and woman, and it took place in the Garden of Eden.

The glorious God never asks a question
He doesn't already have the answer to.

Following Lucifer's act of deception and Adam's treason, God acted swiftly in both judgment and mercy. The serpent was cursed by losing his extremities and being forced to slither in the dust on his belly. He also received a promise of judgment from the future seed of the woman—a future King and Messiah who would restore to them what they had lost. The woman and all of her female descendants were ordained to experience pain in childbirth, and though they would desire men, they would be dominated by them. The man and all of his descendants would be always forced to fight the cursed ground to bring forth its bounty; only by the sweat of their brow would they eat of it. The next thing God performed was an amazing act of mercy. He stationed angels to guard the tree of life, preventing them from reaching out to its fruit, eating of it and living in their fallen condition for all eternity. Then God removed them from their garden home and forever prevented them from returning.

CHAPTER 2

DOMINION LOST

God's plan in the beginning was to give dominion to men, in order to exercise judgment over the forces of darkness! The sons and daughters of men were to exercise complete dominion over the earth and everything in it. In the habitation of the dark forces, they were to crush it down and rule it. Of course, when they rebelled against God, His plan was postponed.

THE SONS OF ADAM

And Adam called his wife's name Eve; because
she was the mother of all living.
—Genesis 3:20

Every human descendent of Adam already existed in his loins. Thus, the decision to accept the original assignment from God was rejected by Adam on behalf of the entire race of mankind. Until the decision was made, no children could be conceived, as God ordained the choice be made to first accept or reject the assignment. After which, the woman received the name Eve because she became the mother of the "living." All mankind came out of her womb.

Shortly after God removed Adam and Eve from the garden, Eve conceived. In the fullness of time, she gave birth to a son whom she named Cain. Eve was jubilant! "I have gotten a man from *Yahweh*!" Is this the one, the one God promised to crush that serpent's head? She cared joyfully for the baby boy. Adam and Eve taught him everything they knew about God, even telling him the history of *Yahweh*'s mercy toward them when they disobeyed Him and lost their royal position, and how He shed innocent blood on their behalf allowing them to live without the crushing guilt and shame. Cain was their little prince, and he was spoiled.

Suddenly, Eve discovered she had again conceived, and when it was time for her to give birth, she rejoiced in another boy. This one she named Abel ("that which ascends"). This child was different. He had great compassion for man and beast and loved hearing the stories about God and His promise of a descendent who would return his people to paradise once again.

Whereas Cain and Abel were raised by the same parents, taught the same truth about *Yahweh*, and had many of the same experiences, Cain resented the presence of this child. At one time, Cain was the center of Adam and Eve's life. Cain had always had his parents' undivided attention and had first choice on everything. But that all ended the day Abel was born. Cain was jealous of this new sibling, and I believe he never recovered from his perceived loss. Abel, however, embraced what his parents taught him about the living God and His requirement for covering their sin. So, he devoted his young life to raising livestock for the purpose of fulfilling God's desire. Cain, on the other hand, allowed his increasing bitterness toward his brother to separate him from God. "If Abel is raising livestock, then I will bring bounty from the earth." He did this, all while knowing God's requirements to cover sin and the process for doing so.

One day, the time of their maturity arrived—they both reached adulthood. Adam and Eve must have been so proud. Their boys had become men! But in spite of their parents' joy, there simmered resentment and conflict. Cain was the oldest and probably fancied himself the hope of his mother; thus, jealousy and bitterness that he felt toward his younger brother only increased as they both got older.

Then the moment came where they were to bring their offerings to God. Abel, in an act of heartbreaking obedience brought a lamb that he had seen come forth out of the ewe. He nurtured it, he fed it, and then he sacrificed it as a burnt offering. As the smoke of the sacrifice ascended, He wept bittersweet tears. His offering was accepted!

Cain, however, in an act of arrogance and self-will, offered God the vegetables he grew out of the ground! This—after a lifetime of hearing the story his parents told of the mercy God extended to them in their rebellion. Even though God required blood, Cain refused, so God rejected his offering.

What Cain did, was not a random killing. Nor was it an act of passion. It was built from a lifetime of bitterness! God's rejection was not the cause but was what he probably used to justify it in his mind.

WHAT! How can you possibly reject what I bring? Who do you think you are? Cain thought over and over. *And that punk brother of mine—what a suck-up. I'll get even with him!*

God reached out one last time to Cain, "If you bring the offering I ask for, it will be accepted!" But God's voice could not move him, and when Cain had his chance, he killed his brother, Abel. What Cain did, was not a random killing. Nor was it an act of passion. It was built from a lifetime of bitterness! God's rejection was not the cause, but Cain probably used it to justify murder in his mind.

When God asked Cain where his brother was, he flippantly shrugged his shoulders and basically said, "I don't know. He's not my problem—or my responsibility." But God knew where Abel was. The very first murder had just occurred, and Cain was unwilling to take responsibility before God, nor was he willing to repent when confronted by Him!

Again, judgment came both swift and severe.

After Adam sinned, he could no longer command the ground to bring forth its bounty. He had to work and produce by physical exertion.

After Cain murdered Abel, the ground that absorbed his blood was cursed by God and would not grow anything. God judged him upon the area of his greatest natural strength. Because he could not grow anything anymore, he was condemned to a life of wandering. He had to *find* food as he could no longer grow his own.

Abel's murder must have created quite a stir in the family, especially among the younger men in the family. Cain must have known that being banished would put his life in danger and cried out for mercy! And God, in His great mercy, protected Cain from death from a vengeful family member, by putting a mark on him and declaring that whoever killed Cain would experience vengeance seven times worse. The firstborn male of the first couple, rather than being holy to *Elohim*, not only failed to obey Him, but also destroyed the one who desired to please and serve Him!

THE SEED RENEWED

> And Adam knew his wife again; and she bare a son, and
> called his name Seth: For God, said, "She, hath appointed
> me another seed instead of Abel, whom Cain slew."
> —GENESIS 4:25

What heartbreak the first parents must have experienced! First, they sinned against the Creator and lost paradise—the constant presence of the Creator, being clothed in His glory. Then they failed to raise their firstborn to fear the Creator. Instead, they raised a spoiled, self-absorbed, undisciplined child who grew into an arrogant, self-willed, and disobedient adult. And, the child they held so much hope for, the one who loved the Creator, and desired to serve Him—tenderhearted Abel—was lost! It was almost more than the couple could bear. Though they had other children, they must have wondered, *Will we have another child like Abel?*

> The firstborn male of the first couple, rather than being holy to Elohim, not only failed to obey Him, but also destroyed the one who desired to please and serve Him!

Then it happened; Eve again conceived!

And in the 130th year of Adam's life, Eve gave birth to a son she named Seth. He was the one God appointed to continue the righteous lineage lost from Abel's death. The hope of a righteous seed was still alive, and it would come from Seth. This would be the beginning of a 1,870-year lineage culminating in the birth of Abraham. According to ancient Hebrew writings, the first high priest of humanity was Adam. This office was passed on to Seth, then Methuselah, and then to Noah. The first descendant of Adam to manifest dominion was Enoch. It was Enoch who poured out his life for *Elohim*, chasing after Him with all of his heart. Like Elisha's pursuit of Elijah, Enoch's heart was so passionate for his God, that he would not leave Him. So, in the same way that God took Elijah from the earth into heaven bodily, God would do the same thing to Enoch. Being the first to walk in dominion over death, being snatched bodily into the heavens by *Elohim*. Enoch was translated into his glorified body about six hundred years before the flood.

This was a period were men were rapidly plunging into great violence and perversion, inspired by the Nephilim. Though there is controversy concerning the origin of these giants, we do know that they were wicked, vile creatures who perverted the earth and caused God to regret ever having created mankind. So, God decided to cleanse the violence and perversion from the earth by means of a great flood. This cataclysm would extinguish all life from the earth. But, "Noah found grace in the eyes of the LORD," (Genesis 6:8). He was tasked by God to build a massive ark of gopher wood and bitumen (tar) which would make it strong, flexible, and waterproof—qualities required for it to survive the turbulent seas carrying such incredible weight.

Before this flood had occurred, it had not even rained. Therefore, when Noah started building this massive structure and preaching of God's coming judgment, they probably thought he was crazy. Where would this water come from? How would he get all the animals in the ark? Nevertheless, in spite of the criticism, he completed the ark and got all of the animals in the ark. When that was done, just as He promised, God closed the ark door behind him, and then the judgment began.

THE HIGH PLACES

So, why did the flood waters of the first global judgment have to cover the highest mountains? For two reasons: to ensure the water destroyed all life and to destroy the "high places." The high places, as places of worship, were important to both God and Lucifer and were either dominated by righteous kings submitted to the authority of the most high God or by the unrighteous allied with false gods. God never appointed His angels—but men—to throw down or destroy these altars to false gods. The angel's purpose is to serve and assist us but never to do what we were created to do!

Today these high places are important to our enemies because of the legal authority they represent. The issue on the earth is who will "say so." Every time obedience is taught to our children and enforced, a high place (altar to the enemy) is being torn down. Every time the wiles of ungodly men and woman are defeated, high places are torn down, and the authority of God is enforced. This is why religion without a relationship with the living God was criticized by *Yeshua*. It is fitting that we refer to Jesus here as *Yeshua* because it is in breaking down strongholds that He clearly demonstrates His identity as "Deliverer" and "Savior." Only the royal descendants of the King can throw down a high place and liberate His children. Mere morality or godless religion could never accomplish this as there is no power or authority in it. Just as the minarets on mosques are high places to the moon god *Allah*, the Tower of Babel was Nimrod's attempt to create a super high place for a new one-world religion. Whatever the usurper controls he must relinquish to a king whose mission it is to enforce the authority of the King of kings. A usurper is any spiritual power (or physical power in alignment with dark forces) that exercises or attempts to exercise authority over anything that rightfully belongs to the king.

God did not choose to meet Moses on a smooth plain but on the top of a rocky mountain, a high place. Caleb didn't ask Joshua for a "fertile valley" to conquer and occupy but a mountain, a high place! David was known for throwing down and destroying the pagan altars in the high places of Israel wherever he found them. The King of kings, *Yeshua,* (transliteration of Joshua, which means "deliverer") as the prototype of the new race, was incarnated in human flesh. He threw down the representative high places:

» In the temple (man-made religion taking precedence over a relationship with God).

» In people (gave deliverance from demonic control and sickness; raised people from the dead).

» In the atmosphere (spoke to the weather/elements, and the dark forces controlling them had to obey Him).

As copies of the prototype, we have the duty and authority to do the same. However, it is only after we possess the character of the prototype that we will walk in his power and authority. That is, when we make the transition from a prince to a king, we will be able to walk in this! Without maturity, power and authority will destroy us. Too many of us desire power and authority yet wonder why we have neither —not realizing that if God gave us what we asked for, we would not end up as a David, but as a Saul! That is, unless we possessed the character to bear the mantle God knows we would have to possess.

JOB

There was a man in the land of Uz, whose name was Job; and that man
was perfect and upright, and one that feared God and eschewed evil.
—JOB 1:1

In the oldest and most profound book of the Bible, there is an actual historical figure named Job. He was not an allegorical figure but one who lived and walked upon the earth during the period when the earth was divided after the flood. According to scholars and biblical geologists, this is when continental drift may have occurred. He was well-known during his time: a man of influence and power whose name was recognized far and wide across the region in which he lived. The Scripture calls Job "perfect." He was whole and complete, which means there was no bitterness, shame, or dysfunction in his life. Nothing was out of order, and nothing was missing. The result of this uprightness was the presence of pleasantness and prosperity in his life. He had a passionate respect and honor for his supreme God and Creator, and finally, Job was utterly "turned off" by any and all moral evil.

Without maturity, power and authority will destroy us.

Job is another example of dominion in action. Though our standard view of him is that of patience under pain and suffering, which is an accurate portrayal, Job was also obedient to (v. 13), dependent on (v. 5) and intimate with (v. 20) God. He had absolute trust in his God!

> "Hast thou not made an hedge about him, and about his house, and about all that he hath on every side? Thou hast blessed the work of his hands, and his substance is increased in the land."
>
> —JOB 1:10

This was a dialogue between God and a very frustrated Lucifer (for the first time in recorded history referred to as Satan or "opponent"). His complaint centered around God's protection of Job and how it allowed everything Job owned to be blessed and was thus multiplying his life and causing his livestock to experience explosive growth. The first thing God did was create an "intertwining formation of protection" (hedge) to restrain Satan's attacks against Job:

For personal protection on every side of him against attacks on his health and everything relating to his personal life.

» On every side of his household to include family, servants, employees, house, and buildings.

» On every side of everything else that he owned.

The second thing God did was "bless," or "show an adoring interest" in his business operations. He caused an explosive growth in all of his livestock in the countryside where they lived. So, what can the rest of us do to get the same result as Job? Let's look a little further.

1) Remove shame, bitterness, and any/all sin and dysfunction from our lives.

2) Ask God to make us humble, allowing God's Word to make us holy.

3) Submit to God's process of change, allowing Him to bring order, resulting in pleasantness and prosperity.

4) Revere, honor, and love Elohim.

5) Learn to hate and despise evil in every form or manifestation. Absolutely reject it! Never agree with the "voice of rationalization" when Satan speaks to you in the first person. Finally, reject what you see, hear, or think that is not from God! Replace those thoughts with His thoughts, His Word, and everything pure.

We can clearly see that Job walked in dominion—not only concerning power and authority over and against the forces of darkness as a representative of God but also by his relationship with Him. You see, like Job, our *position* with God gives us power and authority; however, our *relationship* with God gives us protection and blessing.

A GREAT NATION FORMED

Approximately five generations later, God called out to a young pagan, an idol worshiper by the name of Abram.

> *Now the Lord had said unto Abram, "Get thee out of thy country,*
> *and from thy kindred, and from thy father's house, unto a land*
> *that I will shew thee: And I will make out of thee a great nation,*
> *and I will bless thee, and make thy name great, and thou shalt be a*
> *blessing: And I will bless them that bless thee, and curse them that*
> *curseth thee; and in thee shall all families of the earth be blessed."*
> —GENESIS 12:1-2

Abram's father, Terah, was originally the one called by God to leave Ur of the Chaldees to go to Canaan, but he only got as far as Haran. Apparently, his lack of trust in God delayed God's work in his family and caused the destiny of Terah to be transferred to Abram.

You see, like Job, our position with God gives us power and authority; however, our relationship with God gives us protection and blessing.

God's plan in the beginning was to give dominion to men, and the sons and daughters of men were also assigned to exercise complete dominion over the earth. Yet, when they decided to do things their own way, the plan was postponed. Later, God called Abram, and God had a people again. God's plans for Abram were to make a nation from him greater than the gentile nations of the earth and richly promote him (and his descendants) politically, socially, and financially. God's plan was to make this nation a source of liberality and blessing to the nations of the world. God's purpose for Abram's promise was the continuation of His promise to Lucifer in the garden. God would bring forth from Abram's loins the One who would "crush [Satan's] head."

> *"And I will put enmity between thee and the woman,*
>
> *and between thy seed and her seed; it shall bruise*
>
> *thy head, and thou shalt bruise his heel."*
>
> —GENESIS 3:1

Up until this point in the history of God's dealing with men, His work had always been through individual family "bloodlines." In the progression of God's work on the earth, this is the first time we see the beginnings of a corporate destiny. Abram was a direct descendent of the line of Seth; however, God called him out of paganism. As is typical of men, Abram's ancestors (after Shem) forgot the work of God on the earth and worshiped and served Baal instead. Then, God stepped into Abram's life and revealed Himself. So impacted was Abram that he served his God faithfully until the end of his life.

Abram continued to grow in wealth, power, and blessing as he continued to trust in God. Even after lying to a pharaoh, he still left Egypt much wealthier than he arrived! The dominion he experienced was not only demonstrated in his material wealth but was later demonstrated in his ability to defeat his enemies militarily during the "Slaughter of the Kings" in Genesis 14. Following this victory, Abram offered tithes of his spoils to Melchizedek king of Salem and was blessed by him. As with Adam, Abram experienced God's presence in a tangible way, but also like Adam, he struggled to trust Him. However, God had a purpose and a destiny for Abram's dominion. It was revealed through 1) God's direct protection, as God Himself was Abram's shield (Genesis 15:1), 2) God's covenant with Abraham (Genesis 15:15-20), and 3) God's revelation of Himself as *El-Shaddai* when Abram was ninety years old and God gave him the name "Abraham" (father of many nations). Finally, after more challenges and failures (Abram's attempt to fulfill God's promise through Hagar, the rescue of Lot from Sodom, and his deception of Abimelech) the Son of Promise, Isaac, was finally born. However, the testing was not over. The greatest test of faith was yet to come.

> *And [God] said, "Take now thy son, thine only son Isaac, whom thou lovest, and get thee into the land of Moriah; and offer him there for a burnt-offering upon one of the mountains which I will tell thee of."*
> —GENESIS 22:2

Though God had blessed Abraham spiritually, financially, socially, politically and militarily, there remained one more requirement for his dominion "mandate." Abraham had something yet to master: could he TRUST God. This was bigger than mere obedience. He did not simply set out on foot to sacrifice Isaac. He told his servants in Genesis 23:3, "I and the lad will go yonder and worship and come again to you." At this point in Abraham's life, he trusted that even after he thrust that blade into Isaac's heart, God would, if necessary, raise Isaac from the dead! As the account goes, Abraham lifted the blade into the air, and an angel stopped him from killing Isaac. Abraham's attention was then directed to the tangled brush where a ram was caught. That was the sacrifice he was commanded to offer instead.

How often are we this obedient
when God gives us the command
to sacrifice OUR "Isaac"?

How often are we this obedient when God gives us the command to sacrifice OUR "Isaac"? We can rest assured that our willingness to obey and trust our Provider will bring forth a "ram." As Abraham continued in life, even after Sarah's death, he continued to grow in wealth, power, and blessing—even being fruitful in his old age, having married again and produced six more children. The "hedge" remained around Abraham all his days and, like Job, he continued to increase and multiply until the end of his life.

Upon Abraham's death, Isaac carried on the tradition of his father, walking in dominion, having confirmed the covenant God made with Abraham. In Genesis 26:12, while dwelling in Gerar, "Isaac sowed in that land and received in the same year an hundred fold return and the LORD blessed him." As it turns out, even during a famine that ravaged the land at that time, his herds and flocks ended up so large, some envious "locals" (Philistines) threw dirt in his wells and stopped them up. So, he just dug some new ones! Even during a drought, increase was a fact of life for Isaac.

This dominion continued with Abraham's grandson Jacob. Jacob struggled with some family dysfunction, but God's blessing was on his life, and everything he touched multiplied and increased. During the later days of Jacob's (Israel's) life, there was a famine in the land of Canaan where he lived with his household. He and his sons went down to Egypt to find food for themselves and their livestock. Everyone survived because of the dominion God gave to Israel's son Joseph—prime minister of the Egyptian Empire. However, Jacob's sons put their trust in man, stayed too long, lost their dominion, and ended up as slaves to the Egyptians. When the children of Israel left four hundred years later, they were a nation of slaves.

In the same way today, the dominion God gives to the sons of men is lost because the words of God aren't enough, and man trusts in the sound of the hissing serpent instead. Lucifer has historical knowledge of mankind and knows their every weakness, the source of their many failings. However, when mankind goes back to the words of Edwards's Self-Existent God, and His Son, *Yeshua*, and obeys it, it becomes a protective armor (the armor of God) to guard us from the lies of the enemy.

FROM SLAVES TO CONQUERORS

When Israel left Egypt, they were a nation of about three million in number; however, they were "great" only in number. During four hundred years in Egypt, they had generations to learn and reinforce the system of slavery Nimrod introduced to the world at Babel. You see, the enemy knows that only one can have dominion, only one can have the "say so." Either God's people will, or Satan will. We can't BOTH have it. Everywhere the kingdom of God is manifested, and God's people have dominion, it is obvious to all! When Abraham's descendants left Egypt and entered the wilderness, they didn't know how to do anything except make bricks, follow orders, take abuse, and, of course, sin. This little pocket of humanity was going to have to learn "Principles of the Kingdom 101" from the Master, so dominion would be man's once again. The first lesson was a lesson of "Favor," when God told the departing Israelites to ask the Egyptian people for clothes as well as articles of silver and gold.

> *And they borrowed of the Egyptians jewels of silver, and jewels*
> *of gold and raiment . . . and the Lord gave the people favor in*
> *the sight of the Egyptians, so that they lent unto them such*
> *things as they required and they spoiled the Egyptians.*
> —EXODUS 12:35-36

The Egyptian households gave the Hebrews ALL of their personal wealth! In verse 35, the word is "jewels"; however, the Hebrew word is *keli* which means "apparatus" (implement, utensil, dress, vessel, or weapon). If there had been a military battle, it could be said that they plundered the nation. However, because of the dominion of the Hebrews, it was willingness on the part of the Egyptians driven by graciousness and the force of favor that made it possible.

The fastest route to the Promised Land was through the land of the Philistines; however, God would not allow them to go that way as they were not yet ready for war against a well-trained army and would turn back to Egypt. The former slaves had some things to learn first:

Obedience

They understood slavish obedience, but God had something else in mind. God desired a *willing* obedience. This is the love language of God! The way to His heart is through obedience. This is a first principle of dominion. When God told Noah to build something no one had ever seen (a giant boat) for an event that had never occurred (rain), he obeyed without question.

Dependence

God was their source. God Himself cared for them. He provided food and water for them. Their clothes and shoes never wore out. They were literally provided for by God daily. They woke up, and their food was on the ground waiting for them to pick it up.

Intimacy

This is something God craves to have with us, and we cannot truly live without. Adam (the man AND the woman) walked with God in the cool of the day. The foundation of this is built and based on TRUST! Having faith in God is simply saying that we trust Him. God Himself led them through the wilderness. He was a pillar of cloud by day and a pillar of fire by night.

THE TEST OF TRUST

> *And they returned from searching of the land after forty days*
> *... and Caleb stilled the people before Moses, and said, "Let us*
> *go up at once and possess it; for we are well able to overcome*
> *it." But the men that went up with him said, "We be not able*
> *to go up against the people; for they are stronger than we."*
> —NUMBERS 13:25, 30-31

Every covenant God makes with the sons of men requires a test of trust. God has asked everyone since the creation, "Do you trust me?"

» Adam's was the "Test of Two Trees." Would they trust God enough to eat of the tree of life and thus receive the uncreated life of God? Or would they instead eat of the tree of the knowledge of good and evil and receive the knowledge of their own souls to the exclusion of God's uncreated life?

» Job's was the "Test of Grievous Loss." Would he continue to trust his God even after losing everything he owned—including his children and his health?

» Abraham's was the "Test of the Sacrifice." Would he trust God by sacrificing Isaac, in accordance with God's requirement?

» Isaac's was the "Test of the Wells." Would he trust God to stay put during a drought and a famine when there was no water save what he was able to uncover from the ground by digging?

» Jacob's was the "Test of the Angry Brother." Would he go forth from Peniel knowing that Esau was on his way with four hundred men to kill him?

» Joseph's was the "Test of Bondage." Would he continue to trust God through the years of unjust bondage and imprisonment?

The children of Israel would be the beginning of something brand new in the plan and purpose of God. Prior to this, God always worked with and through individuals, now He had a people, a corporate entity to work with and through. How would God test their trust, and would they have faith and pass the test? The next great test of faith would be the "Test of the Giants."

For four hundred years, the children of Israel had been slaves to the Egyptian Empire. So, they formed the mindset of a slave. They grew accustomed to abuse at the hands of their captors. Their minds grew dull from fatigue by the constant labor, And, the most insidious evil was their dependence on the governmental system! They depended on it for housing, food, clothing—everything. So, when God set them free, they had to be reeducated to learn the way of His kingdom.

The first thing God did for this newly freed people was to reveal their identity of dominion by having them plunder the Egyptians. The next thing He did was reveal His awesome power to them by parting the Red Sea and having them walk across it on dry land (they didn't even have muddy shoes) and in the process destroy the military might of the Egyptians. He then showed them how He would provide for them. They had food to eat, they had water to drink, and their clothes and shoes supernaturally did not wear out. They had shelter, and they were taught the basics of how to follow Him. He provided a pillar-shaped cloud during the day and a pillar-shaped fire at night.

Their dependence on Egypt (the government) would eventually be replaced by a dependence on God who also gave instructions for a mobile worship facility, a place where they could meet with Him and have a relationship with him. More-over, He provided a kingdom framework, a new social order, and systems of law, government, morality, finance, and religion.

During this time, Moses complained to God about how difficult it was to carry the leadership load of so many people, so God told him to bring seventy elders to the mobile worship facility called the tent of meeting. God then took some of the anointing that was on Moses and put it on them. When this happened, the sixty-eight men who were at the tent prophesied—and two men who were not there, but were in the camp somewhere, also prophesied! This greatly alarmed the zealous young Joshua, who encouraged Moses to stop them from prophesying. Moses responded in Numbers 11:29, "Would God that *all* the LORD's people were prophets, and that the LORD would put his spirit upon them." The heart of God craved an expression of dominion on the earth! This was not only a desire of Moses, but it was a passionate expression of God's heart.

Within a few months, the great nation was at the bank of the Jordan River, at Kadesh-barnea, preparing to cross. Moses sent twelve spies into the Promised Land to scout the land. After exploring, they returned to Moses. On the way, they stopped at a brook called Eschol and cut a cluster of grapes from a vine. It was so large and so heavy that two men had to carry it on a staff between them. It was indeed a rich and fruitful land! However, when the twelve returned to give a report, instead of emphasizing the beauty and richness of the land, they pointed to the challenges presented. They would have to contend with the descendants of Anak aka giants! If they were going into the land alone, it would be a daunting task, risking their lives and the lives of their children, but they were going in backed by the all-powerful and everlasting God! Joshua and Caleb gave Moses and the people great news: "Hey, guys, it's a rich and fertile land, and God is GIVING it to us!" The ten scouts gave Moses and the people only bad news: "There are these giants you see, and they are going to KILL us if we try to go in there . . . and not just us, but our children!"

Good grief! The "Test of the Giants" was a miserable failure as that generation of the children of Israel NEVER made it into the Promised Land, but instead wandered in the Arabian Desert for forty years until that generation was dead. That even included Moses. Nevertheless, after the generation that failed the "Test of Trust" died, their children, who by the way, were the excuse for not going in, were the ones who (led by Joshua) went in and took it.

THE CHILDREN OF DOMINION

> *"Moses my servant is dead; now therefore arise, go over this Jordan, thou, and all this people, unto the land which I do give unto them. . . . Every place that the sole of your foot shall tread upon, that have I given unto you. . . . There shall not any man be able to stand before thee all the days of thy life."*
> —JOSHUA 1:2, 4, 6

Dominion is always contingent on movement—FORWARD movement—in obedience to God, in dependence on Him, and through intimacy with Him! He didn't say, "The land will be mine," but, "I have given to YOU." Moses' death initiated a new order. Whereas Moses brought law, government, society, finance, and spiritual order, Joshua moved the people forward against the enemies of God. He led them to have dominion over the forces of darkness empowering their enemies. This dominion started with the city of Jericho.

Jericho was a major metropolitan city during its time. Its walls were thick enough to conduct chariot races around the tops of the wall, and from the outside, they were impregnable. Using strictly natural methods, Israel never had a chance to defeat and conquer this city, but God had a plan. The army was told to march around the city seven times (seven is the number of completion) with the Levites carrying the Ark of the Covenant. The manifest presence of God encompassed the city with God's glory paralyzing the forces of darkness. God then caused the walls to literally recede into the ground like a stage prop, leaving the inhabitants of the city defenseless!

When God's people walk in obedience to His words, depend only on His power and provision, and desire and seek His intimate presence, their spiritual enemies don't stand a chance against them. Jericho was a technologically advanced civilization for its time and a powerful, prosperous city; however, because it was a society riddled with sexual perversion and violence, it was a society in decline. The LORD God said to destroy everyone with the edge of the sword; and all of the gold, silver, brass, and iron was to go into the "treasury of the LORD." This was going to be a "tithe" to God. However, there was ONE person who was disobedient—a man by the name of Achan.

> ### Dominion is always contingent on movement—FORWARD movement—in obedience to God, in dependence on Him, and through intimacy with Him!

Dominion over the dark forces and the accompanying environmental issues of our lives can only be accomplished when God's people walk in obedience, dependence, and intimacy before God. If even one of these ingredients is missing, dominion is not possible. It is impossible to walk in God's assignment for your life without this kind of relationship with God. Achan, in an insane act of rebellion, lusted after a golden image and decided that the rules didn't apply to him. So, he took the gold and buried it under his tent. Ai, the next on the military conquest itinerary, was a little town. It was so small that Joshua told his commander to take a small detachment of men to destroy it. Well, the disobedience of one brought a curse on the entire nation, and this little town caused the death of thirty-seven soldiers—all because one man chose to be disobedient. Once Achan and his family had been severely judged, the army was once again victorious.

As mentioned earlier, dominion always rests upon a foundation of trust in God's ability and willingness to do and fulfill what He promises. It is also predicated on conflict: Joshua's conflict with the inhabitants of the Promised Land was a result of a preexisting conflict with the forces of darkness that God said would be crushed by a man. This is why *Yeshua* said Matthew 10:34 (author paraphrase), "I do not bring peace, but a sword." The call of the kingdom of God is to "occupy" the land that He has already given to us.

> Conquering mountains is not only a young man's game but something any of us can do!

God gave the earth to Adam; all he had to do was accept the assignment (by eating of the tree of life), crush the squatters (the forces of darkness), and remove them while filling the earth with copies of the prototype Adam. However, they failed the "Test of the Trees," never accepting the assignment, never occupying what God had given them. Joshua's mandate was to occupy a very small part of the earth: from the border of Egypt in the south to the Euphrates River in the north, and from the Mediterranean Sea in the west to the eastern edge of the

Arabian Desert. It was an enormous area compared to what they conquered—only about half of it.

The greatest of all the children of dominion was Caleb! He declared to Joshua, "I am as strong this day as the day Moses sent me (to spy out the land). Therefore give me this mountain." The same descendants of Anak (giants) that he originally saw when he spied out the land were on that mountain. At the age of eighty-five years old, he was still ready for a fight, and at a time when most of us would be in a nursing home, Caleb was fighting his way up a high place to conquer it. Conquering mountains is not only a young man's game but something any of us can do!

As long as the Israelites trusted in God to act in accordance with the promises He gave them, they occupied the land He gave them and lived a prosperous joyful life! But sadly, it did not last because when Joshua and the godly elders raised up by him died, the nation began the process of spiritual decay, until by the end of the period of the Judges it was said of them:

> *In those days there was no king in Israel, but every*
> *man did that which was right in his own eyes.*
> —JUDGES 17:6

CHAPTER 3

THE AGE OF KINGS

And it came to pass when Samuel was old, that he made his sons

judges over Israel . . . and his sons walked not in his ways, but

turned aside after lucre, and took bribes and perverted judgment.

—1 SAMUEL 8:1, 3

SAUL

When the Lord God brought the children of Israel out of the land of Egypt, He gave them order through a system of government, morality, religion, law, business, finance, and society. He ruled as king over them. If they were obedient, they prospered, but when they chose to do what they wanted, they were oppressed by their enemies. God's desire was always "self-rule" under a theocracy, led by God Himself—for them to be kings under the King of kings.

Nepotism, placing our children or close relatives in positions of authority, goes back to antiquity. There is (of course) no record of the venerable prophet Samuel asking for or receiving any instructions from God to make his sons judges in Israel, and as we might expect, the results were disastrous! His sons allowed themselves to be influenced by wealthy people who did not desire to serve God or honor His authority. They instead turned the power and influence of their position into a means of personal gain. The disgrace this brought upon the position gave ungodly people an excuse to reject the theocracy and ask for a secular ruler instead. The nation of Israel allowed human failure to obscure their view of the work of the most high God. They allowed their discouragement with men to move them to seek a substitute for God's authority in their lives.

> The nation of Israel allowed human failure to obscure their view of the work of the most high God.

This moment was a turning point in the history of mankind! God had, up to this point, governed His people for the purpose of bringing universal dominion to them. Now, because of discouragement, they would discard the means by which God Himself would form a royal people in exchange for the convenience and ease of putting the responsibility of God into the hands of one they could touch and see. Thus, from this moment forward, God would again demonstrate His authority and man's dominion through *individuals*. The three ingredients of dominion still apply; however, now God would judge the nation based on the performance of the king. Where the king goes, so goes the nation! They would be now be ruled like the gentiles.

When Israel left Egypt, everyone exercised dominion, and they ALL left wealthy. Now, only the king would have that dominion from that moment until the advent of *Yeshua*, the last Adam and the King of all kings.

The first king chosen by God and anointed by Samuel the prophet was Saul. His father, Kish, was considered a "mighty man of power," a warrior, a champion, and even a tyrant among men from the tribe of Benjamin. His power and his ability to project it came from the men, resources, and means he had at his disposal. Saul was the charismatic, handsome son of a warrior. His father taught him the ways of the battle, and the result was an arrogant and powerful young man! This would be Israel's king—just the thing they had asked for. Their judgment had come, yet God was still reaching out to them in love, for the shepherd-king David was yet to arrive. Despite the pride and arrogance of Saul, God still desired to do something in and through him because like the rest of us, God still had a purpose and a destiny for his life.

God put people into Saul's life whose hearts he had touched and changed. God does not send us out to accomplish His purpose for ourselves alone. He will bring others into our lives to be a source of encouragement. Dominion requires obedience, dependence, and intimacy with God, Saul failed his assignment as a king . . . because he lacked all three.

1) Obedience

God commanded Saul to obliterate the Amalekites and to exterminate them completely. Instead, Saul kept Agag as a "trophy" and the "best" of the animals as a burnt offering. Saul's excuse to Samuel was that he "feared the people" rather than God. (1 Samuel 15:2-9)

2) Dependence

When the Philistines encamped against Israel at Michmash, Samuel didn't show up at the appointed time to offer the burnt offering. Instead of waiting for the prophet to offer the sacrifice, Saul decided to go ahead and offer the sacrifice himself demonstrating an "independent spirit." The burnt offering HAD to be rendered by Samuel—he was priest. Saul decided that he was taking too long, so he did it himself! God's glory rides on His order. Saul's interest was in himself and his own convenience, not God's. (1 Samuel 13:11-13)

3) Intimacy

God was a convenience to Saul—not his reason for living. His was a religious worship, not one based on passion, desire, and zeal! God desired a man after His own heart, and Saul was not it. (1 Samuel 13:14)

DAVID

Unlike Saul, David was dependent on God for his direction, and when he received the direction, he was obedient! David was also a man intimately acquainted with God; therefore, was a man who "behaved himself wisely." (1 Samuel 18) He walked circumspectly and prudently before God and men causing him to: 1) Honor the king's authority and 2) Be very careful with his words.

Because David was careful with his words, He was popular with the army he led, including Saul's royal court and his personal servants.

» He found favor in the sight of God Who walked with him.

» King Saul shrank from him in fear.

» He became a man of reputation with a name everyone recognized.

Even when Saul became jealous of David and sought to kill him, David's caution kept him from lifting his hand against his earthly king to destroy him. In I Samuel 26:9-11, David and Abishai went into the camp of Saul after God Himself put everyone in the camp into a deep sleep. David had a choice to make: kill Saul and deliver himself or walk away and allow God Himself to deliver the future king. David chose to honor God's anointing on Saul and walk away, allowing God to bring the deliverance. Even after God's judgment on Saul's life, David honored God's anointing on Saul. Everyone desiring to be a king, MUST guard his mouth as a muzzle and honor authority. Anyone's attitude toward kings caught in trespass and sin should be like David's. He didn't talk about it or gossip.

» He didn't act against him.

» He was heartbroken over his sin.

» God's judgment was not cause for rejoicing—but sadness.

David understood his purpose as king was to lead the people into an intimate relationship with *Yahweh*, thus he built the tabernacle of David. This was an open-ended tent where praise to God could be heard every day around the clock. As the result of this intimate experience with God, the nation would learn to obey Him when He spoke and depend on Him in faith. This desire to please and glorify God's name often required David to meet the enemies of Israel in the battlefield.

Though David was not the greatest parent, he was a very wise king who understood the importance of succession.

Though David experienced highs and lows in his life, God was always with him. When King David asked God if he could build Him a house, a tabernacle made of stone, God told him "no." God had assigned Solomon, David's son, to perform the task. Solomon was the wealthiest man who ever lived when adjusted for the size of his kingdom and the number of people he ruled. Though it would not be David who would build the temple, David made all of the preparations and collected and stored all of the material for the construction. He set up Solomon to be successful during his reign. Though David was not the greatest parent, he was a very wise king who understood the importance of succession.

The next section of this book will cover what I call "The 12 Rules of the King." It will discuss the twelve admonitions of Solomon to his son. It will deal with Solomon's succession strategy and the lessons he passed on to his heir. However, these strategies will also provide great wisdom to us today. They instruct us in how we can walk as sons of the most high God.

THE 12 RULES OF THE KING

CHAPTER 4

THE PURPOSES
OF PROVERBS

To know wisdom and instruction; to perceive the words of

understanding; to receive instruction of wisdom, justice,

and judgment, and equity; to give subtlety to the simple,

to the young man knowledge and discretion.

—PROVERBS 1:2-4

About three thousand years ago during Israel's golden age, Solomon compiled a volume of wisdom that today we call the Book of Proverbs. It touches on many common areas of human behavior and morality as well as living in peace and prosperity. However, the first seven chapters consist of twelve admonitions, or warnings. In the Bible, the number twelve symbolizes God's power and authority. These admonitions were directed at someone the writer addressed as "son" (the Hebrew word ben meaning "carrier of the family name"), in order to continue the generational authority of the king, passed from father to son, from the king to his heir. They created an environment for God's authority and subsequent blessing for the people to flourish as a nation. Solomon's taught his son two lessons:

1) How to be king.

2) How to exercise dominion.

The first deals with the king's character, and the second deals with his authority.

Scholars believe Solomon wrote much of Proverbs himself, but the rest of it he compiled from preexisting sayings and words of wisdom. There are three purposes behind its construction that correspond with three stages or levels of life learning.

THE FIRST PURPOSE

The first purpose is three-fold:

Discern True Wisdom

Solomon's heir was to be able to discern true wisdom and be imbued with it because true wisdom that comes from God is not earthly and carnal. It is powerful. It can identify and then destroy the lies and deception of Satan and the forces of darkness. Though wisdom can only come from God, for us to receive it, we first must know what it is, we must know that we can get it, and then, we must ask for it.

Recognize Instruction

Rather than running away from it, Solomon's son needed to heed instruction and allow himself to be taught and empowered by it. Unfortunately, instruction can only be learned by the pain of suffering. It was truly said of *Yeshua* that He lived a perfect, sinless life. However, as a small child, He still had to learn about EVERYTHING. "Fire is hot; it will burn you. Don't touch it!" or "No, don't put that in your mouth; it will make you sick!" Jesus was two years old at one time, and just like every other two year old, He learned compliance and submission to authority by experiencing the sensation of pain (Hebrews 5:8).

As a result, *Yeshua* was driven forward or propelled by the correction as He grew in wisdom and increased in physical stature as well as graciousness and divine influence (Luke 2:52). However, many of us, because of a lack of parental involvement or our own rebellion, refuse to accept the mild pain of instruction. Nevertheless, in running from necessary discipline, many end up working for a tough boss or worse—thus experiencing a more excruciating pain!

Understand and Declare God's Words

Finally, Solomon's son had to comprehending the meaning of what was being said or declared. The ancient Hebrew writings were originally a part of the oral tradition. In the case of Proverbs, Solomon codified them into a book of wisdom. Nevertheless, they are still "sayings"—things that were spoken or declared out loud. Once we discern wisdom, we must comprehend it with our mind in order to gain understanding.

> Once we discern wisdom, we must comprehend it with our mind in order to gain understanding.

So, what is understanding? It is the ability to dissect ideas in your mind, think critically, and reason logically. King David in the introduction to the Book of Psalms said the following:

But his delight is in the law of the Lord ; and in

His law doth he meditate day and night.

—PSALMS 1:2

The godly man in Psalms 1 did two things. First, he delighted in the Law (Torah). The word "delight" is derived from the Hebrew word *chephets* meaning "pleasure." In other words, God's law is not burdensome to the godly man but a source of pleasure. Secondly, the godly man meditates on that same law. The word "meditate" is the Hebrew word *hagah* which means "to murmur." You see, meditation is quiet, but it is not silent! Therefore, to King David, the Law was not burdensome. It was a source of great delight, and when something is delightful, you talk about it all the time—day and night. You talk about it to others, but especially to yourself. When you meditate on God's words, He unlocks the vault of understanding.

God does not limit his Word to religious or ceremonial subjects, but God provides keen insight into business, finance, government, law, and sociology, as well as theology. The more we declare the Word of God to ourselves, the more we will comprehend it and the more understanding we will gain of what God has to say about us, our environment, and Himself. Moreover, with this understanding, we will also be more capable of synthesizing solutions to complex problems and thus fulfilling our God-given assignments because God's Word (Law) contains the solution (or at least the solution framework) to the underlying issues of every problem.

THE SECOND PURPOSE

Once you "know" and "perceive" by discerning wisdom, being taught by correction (i.e., pain), and comprehending the meaning of things by declaring, the next stage is to seize upon and willingly accept potentially painful instruction on how to be a king. As I've stated previously, all learning occurs through pain. This is either through a physical sensation like touching something hot as a child or through the emotional pain of a business failure experienced as an adult. If you aren't willing, whether by avoidance or rebellion, to receive the pain of correction as a child, it will be magnified to you as an adult by fines, prison, or in the most extreme cases, even death. So, why would anyone willingly accept or embrace the chastisement of pain? Who would be willing to cooperate with this type of process?

People who are willing to endure the hand of painful discipline become introspective. They become calm in the storm and don't allow their decision-making to be rushed but measured. If they have one hour to chop down a tree, they will spend forty-five minutes sharpening the ax. Painful experience teaches you to walk into a new environment or experience with eyes wide open, seeing things as they are, not as you wish they were.

> Cooperating with God during painful discipline develops in us a sense of natural, moral, and legal judgment.

Cooperating with God in this process also develops a sense of natural, moral, and legal judgment. A picture of this is drawn during the dark and difficult years Joseph spent in an Egyptian prison. Though at times he despaired, he never blamed God, and he never stopped submitting to the hand of God's discipline. In the fullness of time, Joseph developed the understanding of righteous judgment which allowed him to interpret Pharaoh's dream.

Once Joseph interpreted the dream and received his promotion, natural judgment provided the understanding to perfectly calculate and plan—in preparation of the dream's fulfillment—the amount of grain to be withheld and stored, the method used to store it, and the logistics of distribution once it was required. Moral judgment enabled him to preserve the lives of his brothers when they came to Egypt for food, instead of exacting revenge for the injustice he suffered at their collective hands. Legal judgment gave him insight into the strategy he used to effectively confiscate the excess grain from the people.

When the famine started, the storage facilities were not opened until the population was hungry. First, they purchased the grain with money. When they ran out of money, they paid for the grain with livestock, seeing they could no longer feed them. After they had given all of their livestock to Pharaoh in exchange for grain, they sold themselves to Pharaoh for grain, effectively enslaving the entire population. Joseph received this knowledge because he did not fight against but embraced God's instruction.

Another example of this is the account of the children of Israel upon their exit from Egypt. According to biblical scholars, the journey from the land of Goshen to Canaan should have taken about two weeks to complete. The only description given by God was that He would be taking them to "a land flowing with milk and honey." However, He never mentioned the desert that stood between them and their promise. Nevertheless, then as it is now, God doesn't take you into the wilderness to punish you. God led the Hebrews under Moses there, He led Jesus there, and He will lead YOU there.

At the Gate Church in Oklahoma City, Oklahoma, I've heard the late Bishop Tony Miller say of God, "God accepts us just the way we are, but He loves us enough not to leave us like He found us." When the nation of Israel came out of Egypt, they had been slaves for four hundred years. To put that in perspective, if they were freed today, they would have arrived in Egypt in 1619. Not only were they enslaved, but they were also dependent upon the Egyptians for everything. This culture of dependence engendered a "small-mindedness" that God had to change. The catalyst for this was the pain of the hot, dry, and dusty pain of the Arabian Desert. However, in the pain and discomfort, the children that left Egypt with their parents finally (after forty years) entered the Promised Land, having learned the natural, moral, and legal judgment of kingdom citizenship.

Natural judgment enabled them to make the ground produce; it gave them knowledge of the growing seasons, the water cycle, the concept of multiplication of resources, the skill of trading surplus resources, and how to create wealth. Moral judgment taught them how to care for one another and form strong family bonds. God incorporated a social safety net that was not intended to create dependence on a man-made system, but on God. Finally, legal judgment allowed them to govern themselves, their communities, cities, and nation. It also empowered them with the righteous authority to enforce the moral and legal systems established by God.

> The periods of greatest divine revelation and instruction occur during our time in the desert.

The corrective instruction of God allows Him to teach us His divine law. In fact, it was again only in the desert after leaving Egypt, in the place of instructive discipline, that God came in the cloud by day and the pillar of fire by night. It was only in the desert that water came from a rock, and it was only in the desert that the glory was revealed to men.

In the desert . . . the place of dryness . . . and discipline . . . and pain.

Like Israel in the desert, God can teach where He chooses; however, the periods of greatest divine revelation and instruction occur during our time in the desert. It was only there that the Israelites learned how to approach God and have a relationship with Him. It was the place where, like Jesus, our identity will be affirmed by God and then tested by Satan revealing our divine authority.

Finally, It is in this place that God reveals to us everything else that is upright and just. It is only during the difficult times of our lives that God can effect lasting change as true righteousness can only be imparted after a series of painful collisions between God's will and our own. At each point of contact, we have a choice to make. Are we going to submit to another's authority or our own? Are we going to listen to the voice of one who has suffered already, or will we try to "reinvent the wheel" and bring suffering upon ourselves? That is why Solomon always equated parental love with physical discipline. Physical pain administered in a loving environment forms children into confident and secure adults. So, experiencing the pain of disciplined instruction will make one circumspect, that is, careful and intentional.

THE THIRD PURPOSE

Proverbs will also bestow or impart a strategic mindset to the future minds of energetic adolescents, especially males (the carriers of the family name). This learning is also for adults who, for one reason or another, were not exposed to these things growing up and, as a result, are in danger of seduction by deceitful people because of their own naiveté or ignorance. These words impart uncommon knowledge, of a divine origin, as well as the ability to formulate plans to bring ideas to fruition: starting a business, inventing something, creating a new app, etc. In short, the overarching function of Proverbs is to teach God's people: first, the Israelite kings, second, the people of Israel, and finally, all believers in Yeshua. All need to know how to exercise dominion over themselves and their environment. That is how to be a king.

> Revelation always demands action, and the process of performing the action is often painful.

There are powerful strategies that must be mined and processed from the sometimes cryptic literary devices used to express them. As you will discover, God is not interested in merely imparting the knowledge of heavenly things but also wants us to understand how things work in the natural world.

> *A wise man will hear, and will increase learning: and a man of*
> *understanding shall attain unto wise counsel. To understand*
> *a proverb and the interpretation; the word of the wise and*
> *their dark sayings. The fear of the LORD is the beginning of*
> *knowledge: but fools despise wisdom and instruction.*
> —PROVERBS 1:5-7

In the Parable of the Talents, Jesus gave an account of a nobleman who gave three servants a measure of silver (a medium of exchange) and told them to engage in trade or conduct some kind of business until he returned. As the story went, upon the master's return, the first servant conducted some business and gave his master ten times what he was given by earning an astonishing 100 percent return on the master's original investment. The second servant also gave his master a 100 percent return on investment. The third servant, instead of attempting to multiply the money he was entrusted with, just wrapped it in a handkerchief and stowed it somewhere. When the boss asked how business was, he just gave him his money back. The boss wasn't happy with the third servant. He called him wicked and then took the money from him and gave it to the first servant. Why did he do that?

First, his master gave him a command to occupy himself with trade. Even though the money was not his own, and he bore no risk, he still refused to obey. Even if he would have increased it by 50 percent and returned SOMETHING, the master would have rewarded him for his obedience. Secondly, God's desire (like the master's) is for the resources that He puts in our hands to multiply and increase. Everything God gives us should always become greater!

» "To know and perceive" is to receive revelation.

» "To seize or grasp" is to learn painful instruction.

» "To give freely" is to obtain strategic mindsets.

Moreover, when intelligent people hear the wisdom of God with the willingness to do what they hear, their reasoning power is multiplied, and their understanding is increased because what God gives to us He expects us to multiply. It's not optional. The first servant in the parable was passionate for his master, so he was passionate about the assignment he was given. Likewise, the same kind of passionate reverence for our God is the first requirement of the intelligent awareness of God, our environment, and ourselves. Unfortunately, the foolish and perverse utterly despise and reject both the revelation of wisdom and the pain that accompanies learning. Why? Because revelation always demands action, and the process of performing the action is often painful—pain that the fool is not willing to tolerate. Instead he or she will pursue the path of least resistance.

CHAPTER 5

RULE #1: LISTEN TO YOUR PARENTS

My son, hear the instruction of thy father and forsake not the law of
thy mother: For they shall be an ornament of grace unto thy head.
—PROVERBS 1:8-9

A dolescent rebellion is as old as humanity. Earlier on, we recalled Cain's rebellion against God by refusing to bring the sacrifice God required him to bring. My own experience shows that this rebellion will always manifest first against earthly authority, starting with parents, and the results, if left uncorrected, always end in disaster.

Solomon gave twelve rules to first, his own sons and heirs—the carriers of the family name—then to the children of Israel, and then last of all to the followers of *Yeshua*. As His younger brothers (Romans 8:29) these 12 Rules of the King are expounded to teach us the authority we possess and the responsibilities required of our royal occupation.

The first rule deals with the relationship we have with our parents. The foundation of civilization is the family, and at its core is parental authority: a father and a mother. One of the great deceptions flooding American society today is that fathers are optional in the home and that families can function in a healthy manner without them. You always hear the success stories of men and women who were raised by single moms (or single dads); however, those stories are the exception and not the rule. According to data from the National Center for Fathering (NCF), in 2012, twenty million children lived in fatherless homes. That breaks down to 20.3 percent of White children, 31.2 percent of Hispanic children, and 57.6 percent of Black children.

> ## The foundation of civilization is the family, and at its core is parental authority: a father and a mother.

The results of this are absolutely devastating!

» **POVERTY:** Fatherless children are 44 percent more likely to be raised in poverty, and 90 percent of all homeless or runaway children are likely to come from a fatherless home.

» **SUBSTANCE ABUSE:** Seventy percent of drug abusers come from fatherless homes.

» **MENTAL HEALTH:** Eighty percent of adolescents in psychiatric hospitals come from fatherless homes and are also twice as likely to commit suicide.

» **CRIME:** Seventy percent of juvenile correction facility residents are fatherless, fatherless juveniles are eleven times more likely to engage in violent behavior and twenty times more likely to be incarcerated as adults.

» **SEXUAL ACTIVITY AND TEEN PREGNANCY:** Seventy percent of unwed teen mothers come out of fatherless homes, and they are nine times more likely to be raped or sexually abused in a home without a biological father.

Why the dire statistics? Because somewhere, sometime, long ago, a son ignored the instruction of his father and abandoned the law of his mother, and the damage continues to this day. Until the obedience of another son somewhere down the ancestral line causes the dysfunction to cease.

As the guardian and physical protector of the household and its order, it is the father's responsibility to provide disciplined painful instruction to his children—primarily his sons. It is the son's responsibility to listen and obey. As the one who aids and protects her husband, it is the mother's responsibility to teach God's divine law to her children. The mother can utilize her inner knowledge of the mysteries of God and how He orders things on the earth, while the father utilizes a more physical disciplinary approach. Together, they make a powerful team.

Though men are not better than women, they are different, and due to generational disobedience and the curses that follow, it is the sons who end up in need of the lessons of maturity. For better or worse, the family name is passed on through the male children and with it, family legacy is established. So, what do the sons need to do to receive, learn, and live out these rules? They must embrace Rule #1:

First, listen to and learn from the painful past lessons of your father. These are lessons that he or his father suffered in order to learn. Hear the lessons with the intention of learning something and then doing what you learned. Also, don't cop an attitude when your father brings corrective discipline to help you to learn. Remember, only *sons* receive discipline—*bastards* do not! (Hebrews 12:8) This recalls an episode of painful corrective discipline in my own life.

In 1969, while vacuuming the living room carpet, I discovered that our pet dachshund made a funny howling sound when the vacuum cleaner got too close to her. Well, I decided to use the vacuum cleaner to amuse myself with her terrified howls. Unfortunately for me, things ended badly when my father happened to walk into the house and discover my cruelty. He decided to immediately apply the board of education to the seat of knowledge. In other words, my father's "instruction" was swift and decisive . . . and painful! It was a critical life lesson as there is a short distance between tormenting a dog and tormenting a person weaker than you. The latter will bring a curse into your life. The happy ending to this story is that I learned from that painful experience and corrected my behavior.

Second, do not forget or rebel against the divine order that your mother raised you with. This is what she instilled in you from birth. Don't reject your mother's uncanny ability to read your body language and emotions; it was given to her by God to protect you.

Therefore, by learning from your father's instruction (as painful as it might be), and embracing your mother's order, you will reap a two-fold reward:

1) *You will receive honor and favor from men and authority from God.* Privilege in life is not always about money. Often, it comes from the favor of God and men. Favor is never "fair," so don't ever be jealous or envious of the blessing of God's favor on someone else. When the inhabitants of ancient Egypt looked upon Israel's son Joseph, they only saw a handsome young ruler of means and power. What they couldn't see were the years of rejection, heartbreak, pain, privation, and prison.‹

2) *You will learn to control what you think and say.* Words are powerful, and what you say matters.

Visible favor and anointed speech create the confidence necessary for a future of sound leadership and the ability to exercise the authority of a king.

CHAPTER 6

RULE #2: DO NOT FOLLOW THE CROWD!

My son, if sinners entice thee, consent thou not. If they say, "Come
with us, let us wait for blood, let us lurk privily for the innocent
without cause; let us swallow them up alive as the grave; and whole
as those that go down into the pit: we shall find all precious substance,
we shall fill our houses with spoil: Cast in thy lot among us; let us
all have one purse, My son, walk not thou in the way with them."
—Proverbs 1:10-15

Throughout history, from the murder of Abel until now, young men have been the primary perpetrators of violent crime in the world, usually as a result of living in a fatherless home. However, whether or not this is the case, the mechanism of inducement is peer pressure. This brings us to the second rule which is, in short, "Don't follow the crowd!" As everyone desires to be accepted and admired by their peers, this is especially true of young people. From the time of Solomon, peer pressure is a powerful draw. However, as we derived from Rule #1, the adolescent's future success hinges on the level of parental involvement. The eleven rules that follow are all based upon the first.

The father speaking in this passage understood that, as a future king, his son could not allow himself to be negatively influenced by those who did not share his values. There apparently were adolescents within his circle of friends who were not parented well and ended up involved with an unsavory (or even criminal) element. These were not poor, disadvantaged youth. Rather, they were privileged young people whose parents occupied places of standing, authority, and means. Solomon was telling his son, "Look! There are usurpers in the realm. If you allow them to influence you, they will exercise authority over you—instead of you exercising authority over them. So, if anyone tries to talk you into doing something that you know not to do, remember what your mother and I taught you. Remember who you are and the name that you carry; don't allow anyone to take you down the path of destruction!"

While studying the motivations for joining the terror group ISIS, researcher Joshua Kirsh identified two groups of male recruits. The first group comprised of local recruits from Iraq, Syria, and Palestine (the Levant). These (mostly) young men were motivated more by the political struggles in their localities and less by religious issues. Researchers also found that most of this group had no more than an elementary school education and little actual knowledge of Islam. The second group, on the other hand, was almost exclusively from Western European countries. They were stable, educated young men, many with professions. These young men were in search of "glory and esteem" and a life of adventure and significance. In short, they were bored and in search of meaning!

Whether it's joining a terrorist organization or a street gang, this warning to "sons" rings clear. If you look carefully at Solomon's words to his son, you can see the offer made to young men and what would attract them:

» You can have the power of life and death—by murder. You can experience excitement instead of boredom—at the expense of others.

» You can control people—by enslaving them.

» You can become wealthy—by stealing the wealth of others.

"However," Solomon continued, "you will have to become ONE with them. In doing so, you have to discard your destiny as a king and, in its place possess, the never-ending legacy of a usurper—one who seeks to gain material wealth through force of evil." The words of the usurper to the son were, "You join us," not, "We will join you."

What starts as a search for excitement and relief from boredom will result in certain destruction!

Every one of these things the usurper attempts to seduce the son into doing will individually and collectively bring a curse on anyone who involves himself in the transgression which, in the end, brings death. What starts as a search for excitement and relief from boredom will result in certain destruction!

CHAPTER 7

RULE #3: DO NOT HARM THE INNOCENT

My son, walk not thou in the way with them; refrain thy foot

from their path: for their feet run to evil, and make haste to

shed blood. Surely in vain the net is spread in the sight of any

bird. And they wait for their own blood; they lurk privily for

their own lives. So are the ways of everyone that is greedy of

gain: which taketh away the life of the owners thereof.

—PROVERBS 1:15-19

The conventional wisdom of our day says that if you mistreat someone without a reason or cause, it will come back to haunt you. You've probably heard the saying, "What goes around comes around." While others call it "karma," God describes it differently.

About 2,500 years ago was a dark time for the divided kingdom of Israel. The adulterous love affair they had at the time with the false gods of the Canaanites brought devastating judgment upon the long-separated northern kingdom. In 722 BC, the Assyrian army completed the conquest of the northern kingdom of

Israel. Their unwillingness to remain faithful to God and the covenant created an environment of cultural degeneration. For example, though Israel was commanded by God to, "Worship the LORD thy God and only him shalt thou serve," during the period from the end of Solomon's reign to the Babylonian captivity, they also worshiped Baal and Ashtaroth.

Why did God hate it so much? The short answer, of course, is that the nation of Israel was joined by a covenant to *Jehovah* (*Yahweh*). God was their husband and is a jealous God. What does spiritual adultery (or idol worship) look like? Did people simply kneel and say prayers to a little statue? Not hardly! Images found by archeologists depict Baal (also known as Molech) as a man with the head of a bull. Ashtaroth was found to be depicted as a woman with exaggerated breasts.

To ensure water was available in that arid Middle Eastern environment, the people of that time believed Baal required a human sacrifice to send the necessary rain. Did they take a volunteer from one of the adult "worshipers"? Nope! They were given an infant as a sacrifice. Well you say at least it was humane, right? Let's find out. The idol was a giant pot-belly stove with both hands out with the palms facing up. A bonfire would be started underneath them in its "belly." Once its "hands" were white-hot from the bonfire, the infant would be placed on them. The body would shrivel in half and fall into the fire. All of this would happen while the congregants were singing loud praises to Baal with instruments to drown out the baby's screams.

You're probably thinking, *How were they able to maintain a steady stream of infant sacrifices?* Enter Ashtaroth, the "goddess" of sexual love and fertility. The worship of this false deity would occur through cult prostitutes and sexual orgies. Of course, without modern birth control methods in place, the women engaging in the "worship" were bound to get pregnant and provide a continuous stream of sacrifices.

Did the Israelites completely forsake *Yahweh*? Not really. In most cases, they did something even worse. They just lumped Him together with the evil, perverted false gods that they also worshiped. Judgment rarely comes immediately; sometimes, it seems as if it is never going to come. However, they sowed the seeds of perversion and adultery day after day after day until their worship of those false gods brought destruction upon them. Eventually, instead of feeding their children to Baal, they ended up eating them themselves! They sowed a breeze and reaped a hurricane.

> Judgment rarely comes immediately;
> sometimes, it seems as if it
> is never going to come.

Solomon's words to his son painted a similar picture:

1) Rushing to destroy the innocent in any manner is pointless! It will produce absolutely nothing for you. It makes as much sense as setting a trap with the animal present and still expecting it to walk into the trap.

2) Destroying the innocent is as self-destructive as setting up an IED (improvised explosive device) to kill yourself. Even if you are successful and get away with it and even gain something from it, it will kill you in the end. If you don't believe me, ask the late gangster Al Capone. According to Elizabeth Nix's History.com article "8 Things You Should Know about Al Capone," though he was responsible for scores of murders and ran a $100 million per year criminal enterprise, he died of syphilis at forty-eight

years old, after fourteen years of suffering with dementia caused by the disease.

And, if you were to ask Hosea, "What does the seed of sin look like when it comes forth out of the ground?" he would answer according to Hosea 8:7:

» "They have sown the wind, and they shall reap the whirlwind."

Sin's harvest is always way out of proportion to what is sown. So, the destruction of sin is plenteous.

» "It hath no stalk."

We think something is being gained, but it turns out our life has no structure to hold it up. The blessing and favor of God is absent.

» "The bud shall yield no meal."

There is no fruit. There may be short-term profit, but there is no long-term value.

» "If so be it yield, the strangers shall swallow it up."

In the end, even if it does yield, someone else will consume it. Nothing will be left.

When you join yourself to ungodly usurpers, it's just a matter of time before you are also overthrown and plundered by them.

When you join yourself to ungodly usurpers, it's just a matter of time before you are also overthrown and plundered by them.

CHAPTER 8

RULE #4: DON'T LET ANYONE HIJACK YOUR DESTINY

My son, if thou wilt receive my words, and hide my commandments with thee; so that thou incline thy ear unto wisdom, and apply thy heart to understanding; Yea, if thou criest after knowledge, and liftest up thy voice for understanding; if thou seekest her as silver, and searchest for her as hide treasures; Then shalt thou understand the fear of the Lord , and find the knowledge of God. For the LORD giveth wisdom: out of His mouth cometh knowledge and und understanding. He layeth up sound wisdom for the righteous: He is a buckler to them that walk uprightly. He keepeth the paths of judgment, and preserveth the way of his saints. Then shalt thou understand righteousness, and judgment, and equity; yea every good path.

—Proverbs 2:1-9

As a child and later as an adolescent, I always seemed to gravitate toward boys and young men who "lived on the edge." The guys who always seemed to enjoy mischief and got into trouble always seemed to get my attention. Whenever my wise mother would ask me why I did something that I knew better than to do, I would always respond, "Well, Sam did it." My mother would reply without skipping a beat, "So, if Sam jumped off a cliff, would you?" Of course, the response to her rhetorical question which she asked frequently was always a reluctant, "no." But where does the reasoning power and emotional courage come from when an adult "Sam" (or "Samantha") tries to talk you into jumping off the proverbial cliff or worse, tries to hijack your destiny. Let's take a look.

In the beginning of humanity, faith was necessary for dominion—not faith that God existed but faith that He could be trusted. The fall wasn't just a deception of the woman; it was a lack of faith in the man because true faith is characterized by a rock-solid dependence on Him. Adam's sin was his unwillingness to relinquish his wife to God. A lack of trust in God is what killed Adam.

> The fall wasn't just a deception of the woman; it was a lack of faith in the man.

Solomon, in this fourth admonition, continued to beat the same drum of moral deterrence. "Son, remember who you are and whose name you carry!" How many disasters would be averted if there were a father present to warn his son? Buried in this passage is hidden a cause and effect statement that implies a responsibility on our part to follow directions to bring a desired result. The late prophet and evangelist Leonard Ravenhill once said, "Salvation is free, but our rewards aren't free," because everything in the kingdom requires our cooperation.

Solomon's father, David, once said, "Thy word have I hid in mine heart that I might not sin against thee" (Psalm 119:11). This is the same word Solomon used in verse 1 when he encouraged his son to "hide my commandments." He used the Hebrew word *tsaphan*, meaning "to hide or cover over." This describes the mental process of grabbing hold of a precept or commandment and intentionally planting it like a seed in your soul and then nurturing it to make it grow. It really doesn't matter if you memorize a scripture or carry around homemade flashcards if the seed is getting inside of you to take root. That can only happen when you are meditating on, thinking about, and/or speaking out the scripture.

Whether you are an adolescent boy or a mature man, God can only impact your life to the extent of your willingness to cooperate with Him. You must attentively seek wisdom while also bending your mind towards understanding which is the ability to deduct how things work and formulate strategies to perform them. In other words, wisdom shows you what needs to be done while understanding gives you the how and why. Moreover, if you aggressively and persistently chase after understanding (that is seeking to know how things in your environment work), you'll learn how to troubleshoot problems around you. While also seeking intimacy with God with the same diligence as when you are searching desperately for financial breakthrough, you will finally be able to discern God's presence and, along with it, the supernatural knowledge that only He possesses of you, your environment, and Himself.

It was *Yeshua* who said in Luke 11:9, "Seek, and ye shall find." Just as God desires us to ask for what we want and need, we can rest assured that He desires us to have understanding, and He promises to give us wisdom in James 1:5. He also will give an "understanding heart" to those who ask (1 Kings 3:9-11). It will be the responsibility of those who are going to be the bride of Christ—the spouse of the King—to take the initiative to chase after what God considers important.

What if you tenaciously searched for knowledge and understanding with the same diligence as you would search for the income of employment? What if you diligently searched for intelligence like a buried treasure? If I knew that millions of dollars in gold bullion were buried in my backyard, I would keep digging until I found it!

This was the secret of Solomon's wisdom. The Queen of Sheba was amazed only because there was nothing to account for his incredible wisdom and understanding. Jerusalem was not considered a great center of learning at the time of Solomon. Egypt, the empire to the south, would have better served that purpose. King Solomon had vast knowledge of sociology, psychology, zoology, botany, law, finance, business, theology, government, and law, yet it was not learned from men and storied libraries, but from God Himself. Solomon knew from the Torah (Exodus 31:2-6) that God alone assigns skills, gifts, and abilities in order to accomplish the assignment He has given us. God also protects the intellectual capability of those who walk in integrity and character, and He defends those who consistently walk before him in moral rectitude.

Solomon recognized a direct relationship between upright character and the level of intelligence collected and then given to us by God. "The fear of the LORD" is indeed the beginning of wisdom (Proverbs 9:10). Moreover, He protects us and our households with a "hedge." What does a hedge look like, and what could it do for us? To see that, we need to go visit a gentleman from antiquity called Job.

Our view of Job in childhood Sunday school lessons was as a very patient individual with terribly bad luck. Our adult Bible study lessons on Job weren't much better. He was a man who lived under continual suffering and pain and became patient as a result. This is only partially true as Bible scholars reveal that

Job was a man of great wealth, influence, and dominion. He had a consistent and reverential honor for his Creator, *Elohim*. Finally, Job found all moral evil to be disgusting. He was turned off by it no matter where or how it showed up in his life. The result was that God formed a protective hedge, or barrier, that surrounded him and kept him and his household from the destructive attacks of Satan which caused the explosive growth and increase of everything he possessed.

What can we do to get this kind of blessing, increase, and explosive personal growth to take place in our own lives? Utilize God's formula for continuous increase:

» Remove shame, bitterness, sin, and the resulting dysfunction from our lives.

» Allow God to make us gentle and pious, using His words to transform us.

» Submit to God's process of change, and allow Him to bring order to our lives.

As a result of this pursuit of God's wisdom and understanding, you will not only comprehend how to gain wisdom and understanding, but you will intuitively begin to gain an understanding of natural, moral, and legal righteousness. This is the righteousness that allows society to function properly and prevents chaos. You will then be able to peer into the window of revelation to comprehend God's law and experience its effect on your own behavior, thus understanding what it means to walk in genuine integrity. This will discipline you to do the right thing when no one can see you.

In our last discussion about Job, we mentioned a hedge built around him by God to protect him, his household, and everything that he owned. Solomon said something similar over five hundred years later—except it was in regard to wisdom. When you ask God for wisdom, He causes it to invade your spirit and bring revelation with it. As it illuminates your mind, knowledge is created, and the discernment that follows it will protect you like the hedge that God put around Job.

When you ask God for wisdom, He causes it to invade your spirit and bring revelation with it.

Solomon used some other visuals that deserve our brief attention. He mentioned how righteousness, judgment, and integrity are like a protective fortress around our lives. The rampart at the top of those fortress walls provides a strategic vantage point to identify life's dangers when they come. This will also act as a vantage point to identify life's opportunities as well.

So, what is a rampart? A rampart is the top section of a wall. It is flat and used to guard whatever is on the other side of the wall, whether a city or a fortress. An example of this involves the wall surrounding the ancient city of Jericho. Prior to God bringing down the walls and the destruction of the city by the Israelites, the aristocracy conducted chariot races on the top of the wall. The thickness of the wall and the development of the rampart allowed the defenders to easily move from one section of wall to the other quickly and efficiently. However, even more important than that was the ability to scan the horizon for threats. If a threat materialized, it could allow for advanced warning and the defenders to be alerted.

Like a protective wall, what do righteousness, judgment, and integrity protect the king's son (and by proxy us) from? They would protect the son and heir from usurpers who would seek to acquire authority they have no right to. When righteous men walk in discernment, diligently seeking God's wisdom, the revelation they receive from it will provide both warning of imminent danger and the presence of the open doors of opportunity provided by God. Remember that, by his very nature, the usurper has no authority or power of his own. It can only be obtained through manipulation and deception. In Proverbs 2, Solomon mentioned two types of usurpers, the "evil" man and the "strange" woman. The danger they present requires a very specific response.

Once again, we are reminded of the wisdom God gives us. Once it invades our spirit, it is sensed by the spirit as knowledge, that is the "awareness" of God, your environment, and yourself. This is the occurrence of knowing what you don't yet understand. When understanding is combined with this knowledge (awareness) so that you now understand what you know, then you can successfully interact with your environment using strategies gained from this usable knowledge. This usable knowledge (or discernment) will act as a protective barrier to guard you from the deception and manipulation of the usurpers. Along with this discernment comes what I call "intelligent reasoning." That is the ability of your mind to actively function in a logical, sequential manner in order to come to a rational conclusion.

In verse 11, Solomon said, "Discretion shall preserve thee, understanding shall keep thee." This is the armed security specialist tasked to guard your life. The picture is of military police guarding a critical asset, such as a building or an airfield that is surrounded by a tall chain-link fence with concertina wire at the top and along the base. Your reasoning, in conjunction with your discernment, acts to protect and snatch you away from the clutches of two different types of people.

The first type of person is the "evil man." He is named as such for a few reasons:

1) His mouth is perverted in that he lies, curses, seduces, and deceives.

2) He willingly leaves the well-worn path of righteousness and his companions, whose way was straight and prosperous, to walk away down another path of misery, destruction, and death.

3) He is happy to do evil and travel paths with evil people.

Every male has one primary weakness or vulnerability—the "male ego." This is ironic as it is also part of what gives a man mental toughness and intrinsic drive. It has been unfairly demonized in our modern, politically correct culture since it is part of what makes a man think and act like a man. However, the evil man takes it to a much higher level. He seeks to exercise illegitimate authority over a young man or adolescent by attacking his manhood. "Come on, don't be a chicken. Quit acting like a girl!" Now, boys and teens talk to each other like this quite frequently; however, this is not the banter of boys. It is the harassment of an adolescent by someone much older. It is their attempt to talk that youngster out of something valuable that the evil man wants whether it be money, power, influence, or even sex.

The "strange woman" is named as such because she is a stranger to the young man she is trying to manipulate. She is described thus:

1) She is living a double life, and her language rather than being coarse and vulgar, is smooth like oil and soft as velvet. This allows her to go from "church lady" to "your baby" in one easy sentence. Her words are able to command your attention and challenge your convictions. Her immediate goal is not to get you to change your path but rather your focus!

2) Like the evil man, the strange woman has relinquished her righteous path and walked away from the associates and leaders of her adolescence.

In doing so, she ultimately became oblivious to the covenant she made with God.

3) As she continued to backslide, her dwelling became less of a home and more of a dungeon especially to the men she trapped and seduced putting them on a downward slippery slope to Hell. None that are sexually intimate with her will ever be the same and may not be able to easily attain the path of the joyful life again.

Solomon explicitly warns us today about the sexually perverted, morally twisted, and violent man and the adulterous and manipulating woman. They are in two ways similar: 1) They were both trained and walked in the path of righteousness, and 2) They both willingly departed from that path.

The man:

» Willingly departs on a journey of wickedness, misery, and death.

» Gladly advances and executes moral evil.

» Enjoys being with people who are as evil as he is.

» Leaves true and upright modes of living to pursue an entrenched lifestyle of perversion.

The woman:

» Willingly abandons the authority she was submitted to during her youth.

» Lives oblivious to the covenant she made with God, so that it is forgotten.

» Lives on a downward slide to death and destruction.

» Destroys the men she is intimate with through the vehicle of shame.

Evil men and strange women can be found anywhere. Whether they are a courtier in a modern European palace, an attorney in a Manhattan high rise, or even a member of a rural school board, they are only interested in building their own power and influence. They often wear a mask of kindness, but behind it is an ulterior motive driven by their own personal agenda. In fact, with moral or religious training, you may find them in your local civic organization or even at church. On the surface, they appear to blend in. They sound religious, but beneath the religious façade is rebellion. They can "talk it," but they cannot "walk it" at least not for any length of time. Like fallen Lucifer, they have no authority of their own, so they have to steal it by manipulation or force. They attempt to usurp it.

> Like fallen Lucifer, evil men and strange women have no authority of their own, so they have to steal it by manipulation or force.

Solomon's advice in Proverbs seems to be based on his own personal experiences with evil, twisted men and manipulating women, using their God-given strengths to get from him what did not belong to them. When you have "nothing," you will not see them, but as soon as you gain "something," they will appear. Unfortunately, you don't have to have material riches for them to notice and come seeking. The important question is . . . How can you avoid becoming entangled with the evil man and the strange woman?

First, you can get on the "path of life" with God and travel it with godly, righteous people that love you and care for one another. That means more than just finding a good church, but when you do, connect with people who are chasing after Him and then intentionally "do life" with them.

Then put on the full armor of God and protect yourself, the path you are on, and the people on it. The battle against the "principalities, powers, and rulers" described in Ephesians 6:12 is not just for your own sake but for your children, grandchildren, and those who you lead. The picture here is of an armed convoy traveling through an area known to be occupied by insurgents. The convoy has to always be vigilant and prepared to fight and do battle with the enemy.

The result of walking this upright and morally straight path, with a wise and discerning heart, will be the ability to live a successful life characterized by great abundance and increase. Successful in this context is referring to the ability to operate in the area of competence given to you by God whether it be the ability to lay brick, be a schoolteacher, operate a business, or be a welder. When God told Moses He was going to bring the Israelites into a land flowing with milk and honey, He used that metaphor to describe the great number of cattle owned by the present occupants of the land and the fertile land they grazed on that was useful for growing abundant crops. However, to receive that, it took the obedience and courage of Joshua to exercise his God-given dominion.

There shall not any man be able to stand before
thee. . . . Be strong and of good courage.
—JOSHUA 1:5-6

Those who choose to stand against the righteous (who are seeking to walk diligently before God), shall in one way or another fail. Even those who think they can stand against the righteous in secret will be thwarted and brought to naught by the justice of God. No matter how sneaky they think they are, they will never be smarter than God.

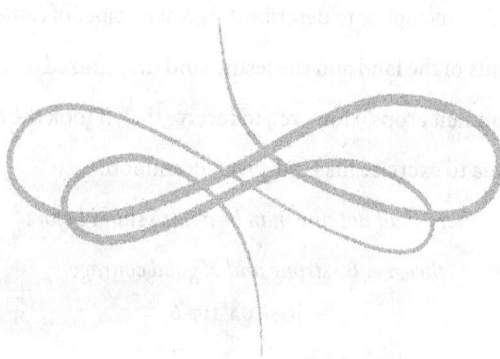

CHAPTER 9

RULE #5: REMEMBER THE "PRINCIPLES OF BLESSING"

My son, forget not my law: but let thine heart keep my commandments: For length of days, and long life, and peace, shall they add to thee. Let not mercy and truth forsake thee: bind them about thy neck; write them upon the table of thine heart: So shalt thou find favor and good understanding in the sight of God and man. Trust in the Lord with all thine heart; and lean not unto thine own understanding. In all thy ways acknowledge him and he shall direct thy paths. Be not wise in thine own eyes: fear the Lord and depart from evil. It shall be It shall be health to thy navel and marrow to thy bones. Honor the Lord with thy substance, and with the first fruits of all thine increase; so shall thy barns be filled with plenty, and thy presses shall burst out with new wine.

—Proverbs 3:1-10

The last rule discussed the danger of departing from the ways of righteousness and our relationships with righteous people. We also discussed how the evil man and the strange woman walked away from God. Though they were taught about Him and knew what He required of them, these "good, upstanding church folks" (of that time) relinquished what they knew and walked away from Him.

> Solomon did not get his brilliance by attending the great secular centers of learning and culture of his day; he received it from God.

It think it bears repeating here that Solomon did not get his brilliance by attending the great secular centers of learning and culture of his day; he received it from God. And his word to his son was, "This is how I did it! So, pay attention to what I'm telling you."

What he said can be broken down into five Principles of Blessing. The first two principles relate to parents, and the last three principles relate to God.

THE BLESSING OF OBEDIENCE

Once while listening to a sermon about the miracles of Yeshua, the account of the wedding of Cana was discussed. During the wedding, the unthinkable happened, and the host of the wedding ran out of wine. Mary the mother of *Yeshua* was apparently in attendance at the wedding, so when it happened, she called *Yeshua*. Their conversation is recorded in John 2. It went something like this.

She told him, "They have no wine," to which Jesus replied, "Mine hour is not yet come." That didn't deter His mother as she immediately turned to the team of servants present and said, "Whatsoever he saith unto you, do it." There were six large containers present, each with a liquid capacity of anywhere from 18-27 gallons. That's a total of 108-162 gallons. Remember that at this point in His ministry, He was an obscure rabbi. Those servants didn't know who He was but understood the blessing of obedience and did what they were told to do. There was no running water, so they had to carry over one hundred gallons of water from a well or stream to fill those containers. It was exhausting, but they did it, and because they were obedient, they experienced the blessing of seeing God do a powerful miracle. No one else but them knew what *Yeshua* had done.

Therefore, Solomon made sure that his son understood a few things. He must never be careless with or forget the things his father taught him. Instead, it was incumbent on him to allow his father's law to penetrate his heart, so it becomes part of how he thinks. Then, when he obeyed it, it could do its work in him. The father promised his son that his days would be "long." In other words, his would be a life characterized by great accomplishment. Not an ordinary life but one lived on assignment. He was also promised a long life. To understand this, you need only know the leading causes of death among adolescents and young adults. According to the Centers for Disease Control and Prevention, 48 percent of deaths between 12 and 19 years old are accidental, and 73 percent of them are deaths caused by motor vehicle accidents. You can find more details at the website under the article titled "Mortality among teenagers 12-19: United States," 1999-2006." How many of these accidents could have been prevented if these young people had listened to and obeyed their fathers and had not been careless with the principles they learned growing up? Many would still be alive today.

THE BLESSING OF REMEMBRANCE

A memorial is an object erected to be a reminder of an important person or event. Some examples are the Washington and Lincoln Memorials in Washington, DC.

A few times, God told the Israelites to create memorials of remembrance. One such moment took place when God stopped the Jordan River from flowing, so the Israelites could cross over it into the land God promised to them. God required one man representing each of the twelve tribes of Israel to pick up a large stone off of the bottom of the dry riverbed and carry it to their camp at Gilgal. There they piled them to create a distinctive arrangement so that when their children asked what it meant, they would have an opportunity to testify of the powerful miracles they had witnessed God performing.

The concept of remembrance was well known to Solomon and understood by his audience as well. The evil man and the strange woman had pretty much the same history as the sons he wrote to. However, at some point, they quit remembering what God had done and allowed themselves to forget. This enabled them to stop walking with God and to walk away from Him instead. They were taught to serve Him and even knew His requirements. They were good, observant Jews until the day they relinquished what they knew.

Therefore, Solomon emphatically told his son:

- » Do not carelessly forget and thus relinquish what you have received. To forget is to risk destitution of kindness and experience its resulting lack of concern for mankind and devotion to God.

- » Keep merciful kindness to people and pious devotion to God in your daily meditations. In other words, think out loud about what God says to you and does for you. Do this until what you declare is engraved on your inner man, so it becomes part of you.

A wise man once said, "If you take care of God's business, He'll take care of yours." Obedience to God in these areas will bring the Blessings of Remembrance, in the following ways: God will supernaturally cause to appear and proceed forth out of you both a bountiful graciousness and success-producing intelligence. These are the two qualities of Solomon that stunned the visiting Queen of Sheba, causing her to exclaim 1 Kings 10:7, "Howbeit I believed not the words, until I came, and mine eyes had seen it: and, behold, the half was not told me: thy wisdom and prosperity exceedeth the fame which I heard." This will happen openly publicly putting you in a position of honor. As the wise king attracted people of power and influence, so can God do this for you as well.

THE BLESSING OF TRUST

In Psalms, King David used the Hebrew word for "trust" batach twenty-five times. He used it to describe Yahweh as the source of his confidence and security—Someone in whom he could put his complete trust! This "School of Trust" began in David's childhood. As the youngest child, David was relegated to the fields and pastures to guard and shepherd his father's sheep. Some Bible scholars even suggest that it was believed by many of his contemporaries that he was conceived illegitimately and banished to the remote pastures because he was an embarrassment to his father, Jesse.

In the solitary moments and with much time on his hands, he taught himself to play the lyre and learned the hymns of his fathers. Caring for the sheep gave him a gentle, compassionate heart. However, when hungry lions and bears showed up for a meal, the worshiper became a warrior! Like David's life demonstrated, trusting in *Yahweh*, making Him your fortress and your refuge, will always bring with it the Blessing of Trust.

God desires for us to walk through our lives with a settled trust in Him on every level. That includes the levels of our thinking, feeling, and ultimately our choosing. However, in our fallen state, we can't always trust our human reasoning. In everything that we do, everywhere that we go, and everything that we are becoming, we need to consider God and His desires. Trust always entails confidence, and when we trust God entirely, we experience an ironclad confidence in Him.

Before Adam sinned and chose independence from God, this was the bedrock of his faith, and it needs to be ours as well. Every part of David's life, from the field to the wilderness to the throne room, was an illustration of an unshakeable faith in God. If we, like David and Solomon, take the time and effort to consider God's thoughts and desires in our journey of confidence and trust, God will honor our trust in Him by causing our path to be straight and even and our lives to be successful. Notice that I didn't say easy, and I didn't say pain-free because success is never easy or pain-free. Moreover, we need to consider God's thoughts and desires. It's only when God's plans become our plans, that we can expect His blessing on them.

THE BLESSING OF HUMILITY

Two thousand years ago, near the Sea of Galilee, Yeshua said these words to a large crowd:

> *"Blessed are the meek: for they shall inherit the earth."*
> —Matthew 5:5

For most of my life, I took this to mean that one day—someday—I would be rewarded for being humble (or meek), but probably not in this life. That is not at all what *Yeshua* meant. A more modern rendering of this verse might sound more like, "Supremely blessed are the humble: for they shall obtain the land by inheritance." Notice, Yeshua didn't say weak—but meek! Meekness is not cowardice, but a certain controlled strength, held in check by self-awareness and the fear of the Lord. Yeshua was the very embodiment of humility, but it was said of Him in John 2:15, "He made a scourge of small cords and drove them out of the temple." That sounds fearsome to me. Don't ever mistake humility for weakness!

The hallmark of humility is a profound trust in God over one's own capabilities. This also applies to our reasoning abilities. God wants us to exercise our minds and be intelligent. Having a sharp and capable intellect doesn't decrease our faith; however, at the same time, neither can that be all that we possess. Whatever rational capabilities we possess cannot stand alone; they must be accompanied by two things: utter reverence to Yahweh and utter rejection of evil.

Yeshua, by His example while in the days of His flesh, taught us reverence for His Father which was expressed in three ways:

> » Intimacy—Jesus would often skip meals and nights of sleep to spend time in the presence of His Heavenly Father.
> » Submission—Jesus lived a life of continual willing subjection to His Father.
> » Obedience—With a life of continual submission His daily habit, a life of perfect obedience was not far behind. This was an obedience based not on religious obligation but on perfect relational love.

Our reasoning capabilities must also be accompanied by a complete and passionate rejection of evil. To find such a stark example of this, we must again return to the wealthy and influential patriarch Job. At the beginning of Job's account it was written of him, "That man was perfect and upright, and one that feared God, and eschewed (rejected) evil" (Job 1:1). Though he was a man of great wealth, it was his character that the narrator found most remarkable and that God found so precious.

» Job was "perfect."

This did not mean that he was sinless; however, his desire for intimacy with God caused him to leave no stone unturned in his pursuit of Him.

» Job was "upright."

He was straight in morals and even in temperament and would not allow his emotions to cause him to sin.

» Job "feared God and eschewed evil."

He was passionate in his relationship with God and hot in his rejection and denunciation of sin.

According to Solomon, in Proverbs 3:8, walking humbly before God in reverential fear and rejecting evil has a profound impact upon your physical health.

1) It will bring "health to thy navel. . . ." The word translated "navel" here is fascinating! James Strong, in his lexicon, translated the Hebrew word skor to mean "umbilical cord," whereas Wilhelm Gesenius, in his own lexicon, translated it to mean "nerve or muscle." This gives the word what I believe to be a compound meaning. The fear of God will give you both a strong connection to Him and a nervous system impervious to the effects of stress on the body. The peace we possess by walking in close intimacy with God will calm our nerves when external stressors threaten to overwhelm us.

2) And, it will bring "marrow to thy bones." Solomon, it would seem, was well versed in human physiology. He understood the importance of possessing copious amounts of bone marrow and the corresponding production of red blood cells. The healthier our bone marrow, the higher the body's red blood cell count, the more oxygenated our blood, and the greater our health and vitality.

Strength combined with confident
faith produces steadfast humility,
and that humility brings God's
grace—His favor—to you!

In James 4:6, the Bible says, "God resisteth the proud, but giveth grace unto the humble." The Master walked upon the earth a life of strength and courage and expects us to do the same. Strength combined with confident faith produces steadfast humility, and that humility brings God's grace—His favor—to you!

THE BLESSING OF HONOR

The first three words of Proverbs 3:7 are "Honor the Lord. This is not a suggestion; it is a commandment. The only other commandment to honor is to "Honor thy father and mother." So, why would Solomon make such an emphatic plea to his son to honor God? To answer that question, we need to examine an incident from the early life of Samuel the prophet.

As a preschool-aged boy, Samuel was given to God by his mother, Hannah. She took him to the tabernacle to be raised by Eli, the high priest at the time. Eli had two sons, Hophni and Phineas, who apparently were not raised by their father to fear God. Eli's lack of disciplined instruction caused them to grow into unbelieving and ungodly men who used the animal sacrifices the Israelites brought before God to satisfy their gluttonous appetites. To make matters even worse, they polluted the tabernacle by sexually abusing the women assigned to do the work of God there. Now, Eli would verbally "correct" them from time to time but would not restrain or remove them. Why? Because they were his sons, and he honored them above God. Honoring men above God always ends in disaster. In this case, Eli and his sons received judgment from God which included the loss of their future legacy and their lives as well.

Solomon well understood that if God's judgment could fall on a high priest, it could fall on anyone. He issued the commandment to honor and glorify God in the most concrete way possible—that is with your material wealth which represents your labor, your sweat and your time that you will never get back! Though Solomon's heir would be the recipient of great wealth upon his father's death, this principle applies to all of us.

Whatever we own, whether great or small, we are to use it to please Him. We are also to glorify Him with the "first fruits"of all our income, revenue, and/or increase. This is not just a salary or paycheck, but whatever God causes to multiply in your hand: livestock, real estate, or business ownership. Everything we have comes from God, so it stands to reason that we show God honor by giving Him the "first fruits." The tithe is required by God, but it is not uncommon to give offerings above the tithe. On a side note, I believe glorifying God with our wealth will cause us to walk in generosity and liberality toward others. An example is when we receive services from others, like when we are served at a restaurant. I believe that stingy TIPs are dishonoring to God, so if you can't afford to tip, then you can't afford to eat out. Honor God with your possessions!

What is the result of honoring God with your resources?

» God will multiply what you have. It will increase until your storehouses in heaven and earth overflow with abundance. You can never "outgive" God!

» Your wine vats (wine being a type of joy) will burst forth and out and joy will characterize your life. This is an overpowering joy that the enemy cannot extinguish, an infectious joy that brings favor from God and man.

LESSONS LEARNED

These five blessings are simple cause-and-effect principles, universal laws of the kingdom. The first one relates to our parents, and the last four relate to God. Again, these are the blessings of:

> » Obedience—When we obey our parents, we are rewarded with a long life full of purpose and accomplishment.

> » Remembrance—It is only by remembering our history with God that we will continue to obey and not relinquish what we have received from Him. This will result in public honor and supernatural success-producing intelligence.

> » Trust—As we begin to see the rewards of remembering, our trust, like David's, will be built up and strengthened. As our confidence in Him increases, there will be a corresponding increase in our reasoning ability, allowing us to successfully walk in our assignment.

> » Humility—As our trust and confidence in God grows and the resulting success increases, we will begin to walk in great strength. By remembering our history with God and trusting Him rather than ourselves, our lives will be characterized by a deep reverence of Him and a passionate rejection of evil. This will impact our physical health by eliminating stress and flooding our bodies with health and vitality. Great strength and confident trust produce great humility which in turn brings great favor to you from God.

> » Honor—When you see the result of obedience in your life, you begin to build personal memorials of remembrance to God's faithfulness in your life. Your trust in Him grows stronger, and your confidence in His abilities is enlarged. Your humility intensifies as you realize that everything you

have comes from Him. It's then logical to honor Him with what He gives you, seeing that it all came from Him in the first place. Therefore:

The more we receive . . . the more we give . . . the greater we honor . . . the greater our increase . . . the greater our joy!

CHAPTER 10

RULE #6: COOPERATE WITH GOD'S RESTRAINT

My son, despise not the chastening of the Lord; neither be weary of his correction: For whom the Lord loveth he correcteth; even as a father the son in whom he delighteth. Happy is the man that findeth wisdom, and the man that getteth understanding. For the merchandise of it better than the merchandise of silver, and the gain thereof than fine gold. She is more precious than rubies: and all the things thou canst desire are not to be compared unto her. Length of days is in her right hand; and in her left hand riches and honor. Her ways are ways of pleasantness, and all her paths are peace. She is a tree of life to them that lay hold upon her: and happy is everyone that retaineth her. The Lord by wisdom hath founded the earth; by understanding hath he established the heavens. By his knowledge the depths are broken up, and the clouds drop down the dew.
—PROVERBS 3:11-20

During Solomon's reign, Israel was an agrarian society. Crops grew in fields prepared by farmers using beasts of burden like oxen. Transportation was accomplished on foot by walking or by some sort of horse- or mule-drawn conveyance. For the farmer to harness the power of the oxen and direct their strength, a yoke was necessary. In a similar way, a horse was and still is equipped with a bridle to control and direct it.

Solomon's sixth rule, after giving the first five keys for achieving royal dominion and authority, now shows his son (and us) how to keep them!

Yesterday, on the way home from church, I passed a horse ranch. I saw three adolescent males running free in the large fenced corral. To the untaught (and ignorant) like myself, it was beautiful and even majestic. However, without the restraint of a bridle and the care of their master, they will never reach their potential usefulness. Oxen, on the other hand, are animals of great strength that are yoked from an early age. The yoke fits them loosely as juveniles, allowing them to grow into it.

As an observer of the times, Solomon told his son, "Listen, do not reject and cast off God's restraint from your life." It is as crazy as a horse casting off its bridle or an ox its yoke. These restraints bring order to their lives and allow them to be useful to their master. In the same way, God desires to bring order to our lives and make us useful in the kingdom. Solomon also told him, "Son, we can never get tired of God's instruction, and we cannot ignore or reject His 'corrective reasoning' (or rational arguments) to us.

Why?

Whoever the eternal God has loving affection for, He disputes and reasons with in a corrective manner. A father treats a son he wants the best for in the same way.

This powerful wisdom actually comes again from the life of King David. Part of what made him a man after God's heart was his unwillingness to take shortcuts to his destiny. When it was time to tend sheep, he tended sheep without complaining about his "anointing" or his "calling." When it was time to be a delivery boy, he delivered food to his arrogant, disrespectful older brothers and never once reminded them that it was he—and not them—that the prophet anointed as king of Israel. Despite all this, he never once tried to fight against the restraint God put on his life. The result of his willingness to bear up under the narrow path of restraint God put him on was a 3,000-year legacy. The future earthly throne *Yeshua* rules from will be called, "The throne of David."

Remember, there is no "shortcut" to your destiny.

Solomon's word to us today is that "It is one thing to receive authority and dominion from God, but it is another matter entirely to keep it." The first key to keeping what you receive from God is to, like David, cooperate with God's process and not fight against His restrictions on your life. The second key is to embrace God's correction. Sometimes when trying to protect my teenagers from peer pressure, I would tell them, "Your friends may, but you may not!" *Yeshua* said in Matthew 11:30, "For my yoke is easy and my burden is light." When we embrace the easy yoke, our life becomes disciplined and directed.

Remember, there is no "shortcut" to your destiny. Only God's process of restraint will get you there. Embracing these things will bring you to a place of intimacy with God as a Father who loves His son and desires the best for him. All true blessing that we receive from God comes from a place of intimacy with Him because, from intimacy, you get what is in His hand. Neither by manipulation nor begging because it is the child that desires the father for his own sake that receives his favor. We do this in our search for wisdom and understanding.

Whenever we seek wisdom from God, God provides it! It's His promise.

If any of you lack wisdom, let him ask of God, that giveth to all
men liberally, and upbraideth not, and it shall be given him.

—JAMES 1:5

Solomon serves as our example. Second Chronicles 1:10-12 describe how from a very young age, at the beginning of his reign, he asked God for the wisdom and knowledge to rule Israel. The end result of this prayer, according to 2 Chronicles 9:22-23, was that Solomon surpassed in wealth and wisdom all the kings of the earth during his time. They came to him from all over the earth with gifts of gold, silver, spices, and horses. They did this every year, day in and day out. God indeed keeps His promises!

The profit derived from wisdom and understanding is more bountiful than the products on display in a silver market in Solomon's kingdom and the revenue obtained from trading freshly mined gold. During this time, gold and silver were mediums of exchange and measures of personal and national wealth. Every year twenty-five tons of gold poured into Solomon's royal treasuries, and with those resources, his ships traveled and did business with the known civilizations of his time. As much as the king traded and as wealthy as he had become, he still recognized that if you have wisdom, you can obtain great wealth. However, great wealth cannot purchase wisdom. In fact, without wisdom, you will not keep the wealth that you do have!

Finally, wisdom and understanding are exceptionally rare and of greater value than the rarest and most exotic gems. Nothing else that brings you pleasure can be considered its equal.

What is it about wisdom and understanding, (or what I call, "wis-derstanding") that is so valuable?

First, it promises a long life. This implies protection from injuries leading to death and from sickness and disease. It implies protection during drought and famine which means continuous provision. This was an amazing promise when you consider how short the human lifespan at that time was. Long life would also equate to abnormally high productivity as well.

Second, a long and productive life will provide the opportunity to accumulate wealth, influence, and honor. This is important because so many children are without fathers which are so necessary for an ordered and disciplined life. Without order, discipline, provision, and security, children cannot grow up to be wise and confident adults. This leaves them handicapped and lacking what is required to accomplish goals, raise children of their own, or start a business. Accumulated wealth passed on to children along with the accompanying generational "wis-derstanding" perpetuate this virtuous cycle. This may be one reason the rich get richer because most families with significant wealth are also diligent to educate their children about money. They pass down the wisdom and understanding from past generations that got them there in the first place. This is also the reason why "white privilege" is a myth. Anyone who accumulates godly generational wisdom will see the result in his or her life. You may not get there in your lifetime, but your children and/or grandchildren will if you are faithful to implement and then pass on what God has given to you.

Thirdly, the roadway of life inspired by "wis-derstanding" is a truly delightful, pleasant path full of delightful people who will desire to walk on that same path. Every one of its infinitely variable beaten paths (branching off from that road) lead to health, prosperity, and peace.

Finally, Solomon called those with "wis-derstanding" a "tree of life." What does this mean, and why is it important? The tree of life is mentioned nine times in the Bible. It is mentioned three times in Genesis, four times in Proverbs, and twice in Revelation. As we saw earlier, at creation, the tree of the knowledge of good and evil and the tree of life were decision milestones for humanity. Eating of the first tree would be a rejection of God's assignment, while the second tree would have been an acceptance of it. At the creation of the new earth, there will only be one tree: the tree of life. The assignment to rule the earth and crush down the kingdom of darkness will have already been accepted by the last Adam (Christ) and all members of His body, born again into His kingdom.

At the end of the age, the citizens of the kingdom will enjoy the blessings of the tree of life as nations. However, here Solomon refers not to "the" but to "a" tree of life—a personal, individual tree. This refers to a specific blessing bestowed on someone who walks in "wis-derstanding." Whereas "the" tree of life in Revelation 22 refers literally to the "medical attending" of the gentile ethnic groups, Solomon referred to a more personal level. He knew and understood the original consequence of choosing the tree of life, which was to bring judgment upon Satan and the forces of darkness. Yet he also had a prophetic view of the future, where a dominion mandate would bring healing to those damaged by the fall and living a life shrouded in darkness and confusion.

Specifically, then, what is a tree of life in this age? It is someone who, as a servant of God and a follower of Christ, walks in dominion authority over his enemies, bringing healing and freedom to those damaged and broken people around him. In effect, it is walking in the same authority and healing power that the Son of God did. This authority comes from God, whom Solomon uses as an example to describe the benefits of wisdom, understanding, and knowledge.

» Wisdom is a creative and innovative characteristic of God.

» Understanding is God's ability to reason and think intelligently.

» Knowledge here is God's awareness of Himself and His creation which is everything that can be known.

As a result of His innovative characteristics, He laid out and fulfilled a perfect plan for the earth. I believe He created it so perfectly that it would be understood by rational thinking people to be impossible to replicate in any other way. It took God's intelligence and powers of reason (rather than accident) for Him to fashion the earth, moon, and stars. By His total awareness of everything He made and how it works, He is not surprised or caught off guard when the tectonic plates below the oceans move, split, or rip apart beneath the ocean deep and the clouds in the atmosphere drop dew down upon the earth. God not only knows about these things, He made them happen.

> By His total awareness of everything He made and how it works, God is not surprised or caught off guard when the tectonic plates below the oceans move, split, or rip apart beneath the ocean deep.

Why are these things important? What does this have to do the "world of men"? Part of being created in God's image means also having His characteristics which includes His dominion. However, in order to exercise that dominion, you need to obtain wisdom and understanding.

» **Wisdom**

God's creative qualities are ours when we ask. They are a requirement of kings to exercise their authority. Again, James 1:5 is the promise, and 2 Chronicles 9:23 is an example of the promise's fulfillment.

» **Understanding**

God's ability to reason and think critically are what God expects for us to develop ourselves. This is not necessarily correlated to a formal education but is something everyone should be able to do. Muscle tissue is developed by being challenged. It is only by the wearing down and eventual failure of muscle tissue that newer and stronger tissue can grow in its place. In the same way, our "mental muscles" are developed by having our ideas challenged, forcing us to think and use our reason, causing us to grow stronger.

The most important aspect of education and learning is not merely the dispensing of information. It is converting that information into understanding by our ability to think. It's not enough to make dogmatic statements and expect to be believed, but God expects for us to prove everything. This not only occurs in fields of theology and philosophy but in every field. This conversion of information can only occur when reason is developed, and it can only be developed through practice. Opposition to our plans and ideas not only occurs when we are set against the schemes of the enemy, and his desire is to slow our forward momentum. It can also occur when God is fighting desperately to keep us from frustrating our purpose by threatening to break the protective boundaries He has set around us.

CHAPTER 11

RULE #7: DON'T BE COMPLACENT; JUST STAY FOCUSED!

My son, let not them depart from thine eyes: keep sound wisdom and discretion: So shall they be life unto thy soul, and grace unto thy neck. Then shalt thou walk in thy way safely, and thy foot shall not stumble. When thou liest down, thou shalt not be afraid: yea, thou shalt lie down, and thy sleep shall be sweet. Be not afraid of sudden fear, neither of the desolation of the wicked, when it cometh. For the Lord shall be thy confidence, and shall keep thy foot from being taken. Withhold not good from them to whom it is due, when it is in the power of thine hand to do it. Say not unto thy neighbor, Go, and come again, and tomorrow I will give; when thou hast it by thee. Devise not evil against thy neighbor, seeing he dwelleth securely by thee. Strive not with a man without cause, if he have done thee no harm. Envy thou not the oppressor, and choose none of his ways. For the froward is abomination to the Lord: but his secret is with the righteous. The curse of the Lord is in the house of the wicked: but he blesseth the habitation of the just. Surely he scorneth the scorners: but he giveth grace unto the lowly.

The wise shall inherit glory: but shame shall be the promotion of fools.

—PROVERBS 3:21-35

According to research published in an article on Cleveland.com by Theresa Dixon Murray, 70 percent of lottery winners end up bankrupt. That is a stunning number! There are several reasons mentioned in the study, not the least of which included gambling, drug addiction, and even giving money away to "close friends" and family. Though many of us have the problem of not enough money, there are those who have the problem of "too much" money. They both (in many cases) indicate a lack of wisdom and understanding.

As the wisest and wealthiest man who ever lived, Solomon understood the difference between mere wealth accumulation and real financial increase. The former is the ability to *get* rich; the latter is the ability to *stay* rich. Lottery winners, athletes, and celebrities have lost fortunes in very short periods of time. However, heirs who ignore the wisdom of their predecessors are capable of squandering enormous fortunes, of which one example is the Vanderbilt dynasty.

In 1810, Cornelius Vanderbilt borrowed $100 from his mother to start a business. By the time of his death in 1877, the "Commodore," as he was known at the time, owned a steamship and railroad empire valued at over $100 million. (That would be over $2.5 billion in 2019 dollars!) However, by the fourth generation, lavish living and poor management took their toll, and by 1971, the Vanderbilt fortune was gone.

Though money is a mere medium
of exchange without morality, it
is a magnifier of character.

You see, though money is a mere medium of exchange without morality, it is a magnifier of character. If you are a wise and selfless person, you will be a never-ending source of resources for God's kingdom. However, if you are naive and selfish, even if you stumble upon great wealth, your only chance of hanging onto it would be to hire wise and trustworthy people to help you manage it.

In this seventh rule, Solomon in so many words exhorted his heir:

"Don't lose your focus; instead, remain 'dialed into' the things I passed on to you, namely wisdom, understanding, and the knowledge of God. Guard your reasoning and critical thinking skills from intellectual complacence. Also, be sure to protect your ability to accurately discern and respond to the intuition of your spirit."

As a result of this focus, our souls will stay fresh and alive causing our meditations and speech to be kind and gracious. This will invariably show up in our actions and our relationships with people bringing favor from them. This will create a continued cascade of effects in our lives:

1) We will walk through the course of life confidently without stumbling.

2) When we lay down to rest, we will not be suddenly and anxiously awakened, but instead our sleep will be pleasant and undisturbed.

With this newfound confidence and peace, even when confronted by frightening life events or when devastation caused by evil people comes near us, we are commanded not to be startled or fearful. Why is this? Because God Himself promises to be our confidence and will prevent us from being caught in a trap by the enemy. Solomon then shifted gears and discussed the importance of integrity in personal relationships. I can hear Solomon's words clearly:

If you desire to be a king, under the authority of the King of kings, you must not . . . Deny or withhold material bounty, emotional kindness, or gracious words when appropriately due. Especially, when you possess the power, means, and/or ability to provide it. Tell an associate or companion to return at a more personally convenient time when you already have what they need and can give it to them. Fabricate secret evil plans against your neighbor while he is living securely and confidently near you. Contend with someone who has not treated you in a hurtful or harmful way without any reason. Desire the power of an evil man living advantageously by violence and cruelty or by beating down everyone weaker than himself; nor should you choose to live like him.

Why are these so? Because God is disgusted by the perverse who turn away from Him. Notice I didn't say *angry with*. I said *disgusted*. God's nature, because it is preeminently holy, cannot endure the presence of sin. He is attracted to those who desire and seek after Him. It is with these kinds of people that He holds His intimate secret consultations.

Solomon's father, David, is well-known for some of the blunders he committed as king. In one instance, he decided to conduct a census of the nation of Israel. This was, we discovered, a decision rooted in pride. This one act brought a deadly plague upon Israel, taking seventy thousand innocent lives. Unfortunately, he is more well-known for committing adultery with Bathsheba—and then murdering her husband. If I were God, I would probably have omitted this embarrassing account from the Bible. Nevertheless, God's forgiveness and redemption spans the history of mankind. What made David different from "the perverse, who walk away from God" was his heart. David was in love with God and was a worshiper from his youth. His moral failures were recorded to give the rest of us hope for God's redemptive purpose for our lives.

When David was forced to flee from the presence of King Saul, men came from everywhere to join his band. David was, by this time, a skilled warrior who had been at this point, long ago, anointed by God to be king. However, it was how he lived that attracted them. David was calm under pressure and also upright and circumspect; however, it was his secret life with God that gave his men the confidence to stay with him.

Every one of us has a special talent or skill, but everything we would ever hope to accomplish for God, without intimacy with Him in the secret place, in the end will fail! What we are doing may have all the trappings of success, but without the intimate presence of God in our lives, it will eventually fall flat on the ground.

The conduct of a king is what makes or breaks him—not his title. In the same way, as members of a royal priesthood, we are also required by our High Priest to act like him. It's like Solomon told his heir: If you want to experience the highest level of intimacy with me, then you are required to act by the same laws that I do. "When you act like royalty, you get the reward of royalty which is intimate, secret consultation with the king."

The conduct of a king is what makes or breaks him—not his title.

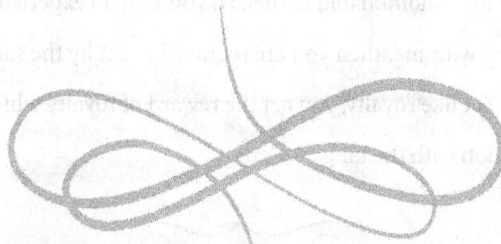

CHAPTER 12

RULE #8: A STRATEGIC MINDSET BRINGS INCREASE

My son, attend to my words; incline thine ear unto my sayings. Let
them not depart from thine eyes; keep them in the midst of thine heart.
For they are life unto those that find them, and health to all their flesh.
Keep thy heart with all diligence: for out of it are the issues of life. Put
away from thee a froward mouth, and perverse lips put far from thee.
Let thine eyes look right on, and let thine eyelids look straight before
thee. Ponder the path of thy feet, and let all thy ways be established.
Turn not to the right hand nor to the left: remove thy foot from evil.
—Proverbs 4:20-26

As we have discussed in past chapters, God's desire for us is that we walk in dominion. It was His desire for man in the beginning just as it is today. One critical component of this characteristic deals with increase. This is not just referring to money (in fact, money is probably the least important aspect of increase). Rather, I would propose, the knowledge of God is the key to increase in our lives. If we allow God to increase the flow of knowledge in our lives, money will never be in short supply. The acquisition of it will not be the most important thing on our minds but merely a by-product or result of operating in the knowledge that God reveals to us. To see what increase looks like, let's go back to Genesis.

Genesis 26 begins with an enormous problem. The land is unable to produce. This was catastrophic for an agrarian society that relied on the proper amount of rainfall in its season to ensure an adequate grain harvest for man and beast. So, what caused this lack? There had been no rain.

Now, Isaac's first thought was to go south to Egypt and the water supply of the mighty Nile River. To Isaac, whose only thought was keeping his family and cattle alive, this was a "no-brainer." Egypt is a type of world system, and for most of us, the temptation is to lean on that system when problems arrive. His thought processes were no different than many of us today, but God had other plans. He told Isaac to "Stay Put!" Like his father before him, He was reluctant to stay; nevertheless, his trust in God and the corresponding obedience brought God's increase. Though there was no indication of any miraculous or supernatural intervention, Isaac, nevertheless, knew where to plant. The knowledge of God is a primary requirement for exercising dominion on the earth. Isaac did not randomly pick a field and plant grain; he knew exactly where to plant! The knowledge of God is not merely religious knowledge *about* God; instead, it is knowledge that God possesses. We can't have all of it, or we would be omniscient, but we can possess knowledge that our individual assignments require. Of course, Isaac knew where the water was before he started digging. God's blessing on him was merely His seal of approval on what Isaac was doing.

Let's review:

» There was a famine in the land caused by a drought which means no rain.

» There was no water to be found, so food could not grow.

» Grain used to feed people and livestock was running out.

» Catastrophe was looming.

» Isaac found a water source when no one else could and reaped one hundred times more grain than he sowed into the ground.

If Isaac had sown one hundred pounds of seed, he would have reaped ten thousand pounds of grain. If he then sowed 10 percent of his harvest (one thousand pounds) as seed, he would reap one hundred thousand pounds of grain. If he sowed 10 percent of that harvest as seed (ten thousand pounds), he would reap one million pounds of grain! The result would be fairly predictable if this continued.

The Philistines, in their desperation to keep themselves, their households, and their cattle alive, probably began trading the assets they possessed for grain. In times of desperation and fear, people often tend to accept mediums of exchange and rates that they would, in much better times, reject. Thus Isaac, by strategic thinking and shrewd business deals, became extremely wealthy in a very short time. As his flocks, herds, and servant staff increased, so did his water requirements. However, though he knew where he could get more water (his father's old wells), the public outcry against Isaac forced him to leave his land. Even though the knowledge of God enabled him to find more water on that land, the Philistines, again, forced him off the land.

In this eighth rule, Solomon communicated three essential principles to his heir:

1) "My words are powerful and have life, so pay close attention to them. In fact, they are so important to your emotional and physical well-being that

you must remember them." In this way, Abraham's words were powerful to Isaac as Abraham knew where the natural springs were located. If Isaac had not carefully listened, he may well have perished along with the Philistines. The memories of what he learned from his father allowed him to not only live—but thrive.

2) "Keep the spring of your soul unobstructed and pure, so that the knowledge of God can flow out of it. Guard it with your life as you would a strategic military asset by refusing to pollute it by allowing anything impure to come out of it." (also see Matthew 15:11 and Ephesians 5:1) Except for a generational weakness (lying when under pressure), Isaac was a righteous man who understood the importance of his words. This was demonstrated by how he spoke to others, especially by those in authority.

3) "Think strategically and take the 'long view' of things. Don't just look at the next quarter or fiscal year; rather, look at how your decisions will impact your children and grandchildren and future generations. Calculate the long-term benefits and consequences of your decisions." (also see Luke 18:28-30)Solomon used a physical structure to draw this illustration. During his time, walls were built around cities for protection from an attack by a hostile military or criminal force. The soldiers that stood guard, were posted at a place on the top of the wall called a rampart. Their attention most of the time was not at the base of the wall but on what was happening miles away. Not on what was near them but on what was coming in order to have the time to prepare for its arrival. The rampart had to be flat and smooth, so soldiers could quickly move their resources to where they were needed. In the same way, our strategy cannot be static. It must be agile, allowing us to shift our resources as necessary.

Isaac understood early on that he had resources no one else possessed, and he saw the huge strategic advantage he possessed. With a secure and abundant water supply, Isaac was able to quickly build a substantial surplus of grain in the middle of a famine. It was like having a license to print money during an economic depression. It is during times like this that fortunes are made because "luck favors the prepared." During these periods, with risk of loss so high, loans are hard to get. This in turn causes the demand for everything to drop, and along with demand, prices. Therefore, those with surplus cash are positioned to purchase hard assets (property, buildings, and equipment), things that will increase cash flow, for pennies on the dollar.

Isaac did something very similar during the famine. In an agrarian environment, the most important thing is to have enough food (in this case grain) to eat, then enough for the animals, flocks, and herds, then enough to sell. During a drought, depending on severity, your priority becomes staying alive until you can find water to irrigate and start planting again. As grain was in short supply and Isaac was the only source of supply, the cost showed a corresponding increase. Now, as a medium of exchange, its value would have skyrocketed (very high demand for a limited resource) as the flocks of goats and sheep and the yokes of oxen became a liability to the Philistines, consuming the limited supply of water and grain. The demand for these things dropped along with the prices, allowing Isaac to buy productive "hard assets" at fire sale prices. This strategy allowed Isaac to become very rich very quickly!

Following God's promise to Isaac in Genesis 26:4, and his corresponding decision to trust God instead of the economic power of Egypt, Isaac decided to trust his own reasoning capabilities. Rather than trust God to fulfill His purpose for him by supernaturally protecting him, Isaac lied to the Philistines by calling Rebekah his sister. Now, from a reasoning perspective, Isaac probably remembered the story about his parents, and how his father's lie to a much younger version of the Philistine king (Abimelech) brought him to a substantial windfall of livestock, servants, and land. Nevertheless, Isaac's memory failed him, but not Abimelech; the elderly king sharply rebuked Isaac for his dishonesty and gave him nothing.

Isaac was a righteous and moral man, but lying to the Philistines at Gerar by claiming Rebekah was his sister could have brought a curse upon the entire nation if even one man had taken Rebekah as his wife. Fortunately for the Philistines, Isaac could not keep his hands off her, and his lie was uncovered. God again used a gentile ruler to bring correction to a child of promise, and this time, God's man got nothing until he started sowing seed. Fallen humanity's natural tendency is to try to get something for nothing, but God's way is through the process of sowing and reaping. God doesn't provide a piece of fruit from a seed. He provides it from a fruit tree. Though His plan for us is multiplication and increase, He will never do it at the expense of our character.

> Though His plan for us is multiplication and increase, He will never do it at the expense of our character.

Having the knowledge of God allowed Isaac to become very wealthy; however, it didn't protect him from inevitable conflict. We can't be surprised, and we can't allow ourselves to become bitter when we lose the battles for the wells that we dig. When this happens, we need to already be in the habit of digging new wells. During both Isaac's and Solomon's times, wells provided water for people to drink in addition to their livestock and crops. Today (at least in the Western world), you don't have to dig because you get your drinking water from a faucet. However, your business can still go bankrupt, you could get laid off from your job, and as a young person, you could be cut from your high school sports team. However, you must never give up and never quit! It was Isaac's persistence that eventually caused his enemies to approach him and ask for a peace treaty. You see, even after he left Gerar and the land of the Philistines, he continued to increase until he became not only an economic threat to them but a military threat as well. And it was all because the wells he continued to dig gave him a strategic advantage as they will give us as well.

CHAPTER 13

RULE #9: EMBRACE CORRECTION

My son, attend unto my wisdom, and bow thine ear to my understanding: That thou mayest regard discretion, and that thy lips may keep knowledge. For the lips of a strange woman drop as an honeycomb, and her mouth is smoother than oil: But her end is bitter as worm-wood, sharp as a two-edged sword. Her feet go down to death: her steps take hold on hell. Lest thou shouldst ponder the path of life, her ways are moveable, that thou canst not know them. Hear me now therefore, O ye children and depart not from the words of my mouth, Remove thy way far from her, and come not nigh the door of her house: Lest thou give thine honor unto others, and thy years unto the cruel: Lest strangers be filled with thy wealth: and thy labours be in the house of a stranger: And thou mourn at the last, when thy flesh and thy body are consumed, And say, "How have I hated instruction, and my heart despised reproof."
—PROVERBS 5:1-12

In the purposes of God, kings and queens—from the beginning—were always intended to rule together because the way of the kingdom is neither a patriarchal nor matriarchal system. They were to govern the same way God desired the first couple to do, which was together. It is the king's responsibility to govern his area of dominion, and it is the queen's responsibility to aid in this responsibility. However, her most important job is to protect the king against usurpers. The king protects the realm from external public enemies while the queen protects the king from internal secret ones.

For a time, during the period of the divided kingdom, the northern kingdom (Israel) was ruled by King Ahab. It was said of Ahab that he, "Fearlessly and brazenly lived a life of public debauchery." As a Hebrew, he knew what the Law required of him. Yet, without a relationship with the Law Giver, it became easy for him to ignore the law he was taught as a child. As he matured into adulthood, he then discovered the cultural equivalent of the "swinger's lifestyle," which, during his time, was the worship of Ashtoreth. As earlier mentioned, this involved ritual prostitution and orgies. Ahab vigorously embraced this lifestyle and pursued it relentlessly. This also included the worship of Baal and the ritual slaughter of babies born out of these idolatrous unions. Then, to make it even worse, as if it were no big deal, Ahab married a Phoenician princess by the name of Jezebel. For Ahab, the worship of Baal was not only a way to ensure abundant rain and bountiful harvests, but it was fun and fashionable (if not gruesome) and a way to be rid of all those "inconvenient" babies.

Of course, when Jezebel appeared on the scene, everything changed. As you could probably imagine, Jezebel did not consider Baal worship a fashionable religion to practice for her personal amusement. For her, it was neither fashionable nor amusing. The worship of Baal and his cohort Astaroth was, for her, deadly serious business. Her father, the king-priest of Tyre and Sidon, was named

Eth-Baal which means "with Baal." Her own name Jezebel meant "chaste," which indicates she may have been dedicated as a virgin to Baal. Rather than protect her husband the king against usurpers, she became the usurper she was supposed to protect him from. His unwillingness to follow the wisdom of his fathers and live righteously before God made him an easy target to a priestess of Baal who had been dedicated to him from childhood.

The Jezebel spirit found its origin in Semiramis, the mother of Nimrod, who was expressed in society as the "strange woman" of Proverbs. Jezebel's focus was the glorification of Baal. This included the cultural and religious conquest of Israel with Baal instead of *Yahweh* ascendant. As a "strange woman" herself, her focus was power, and her method was to usurp it from Ahab using manipulation and control. Being weak in character and a prisoner of corrupt behavior left Ahab exposed and unable to stand up to the strategies of Jezebel. As a result, she was able to exploit this political and moral vacuum and maneuver the levers of power in Ahab's kingdom. This allowed her to eliminate her enemies which included the prophets of *Yahweh*. She even pressured her husband (to the point of physical exhaustion) to build altars to Baal and Ashtaroth.

Peering through the lens of time, Solomon was able to discern the arrival of Jezebel, and other women like her. When warning of her arrival, he urged his heir, saying: "Listen carefully to what I'm saying to you! Hear my wise and intelligent arguments in order to carry them out yourself."

What was Solomon's concern, and what does it matter for us today? The shrewd discernment he was trying to instill in his heir was going to protect him from usurpers in two ways:

    1) It would allow him (and by proxy, you) to carefully guard what he said so as not to reveal critical personal strategies to the wrong people.

2) It would allow him (and by proxy, you) to accurately assess people's motives and desires to maximize their strategic advantage and to minimize yours.

Why are these things so important to accomplish? If you remember, the "strange woman" is a woman willing to turn aside to give personal attention to a man who is neither her husband nor even her fiancé. She is willing to serve a man in a way that would be considered below her in order to obtain something he possesses.

This woman will not immediately try to draw your attention by dressing immodestly. She is much too strategic for that and would never "tip her hand" by being so blatant. Instead, she uses subtle emotionally and sexually attractive language to cause you to drop your mental guard, to enable her to seduce her way into your life. She wants what you have, whether it is wealth, power, or influence. To obtain it, she will attempt to destroy your life and legacy on three levels:

1) She will destroy the peace of your home so that it is no longer a sanctuary.

2) She will devalue and destroy your manhood with severe and destructive words.

3) She will constantly put more financial demands on you until your health is affected, resulting in your early death.

4) Considering this, we all need to evaluate direction in life and choose our path accordingly. What makes the strange woman so dangerous is that her strategies are always evolving to stay ahead of you, to prevent you from recognizing them. This is a formidable power that depends on your character weakness and lack of discernment for her to find an opening and gain a foothold. The brazen sin of Ahab provided a wide-open door.

Once you recognize the strange
woman, stay far away from her,
and don't try to outsmart her.

Pay attention, then, and listen to people who give wise counsel. Don't tune them out! Once you recognize the strange woman, stay far away from her, and don't try to outsmart her. You will lose. Stay away from her house, apartment, or hotel room so that you don't end up forfeiting whatever wealth, power, or legacy you possess—not to mention the time and effort that it took to get you there. You don't want someone else enjoying the fruit of your labor. Not only that, but everything that was yours will end up being controlled by her until, finally, you find yourself a stranger in your own house.

You will likely end up in a loveless, passionless, sexless marriage watching helplessly as your resources are utterly consumed. After which you will finally realize:

All this misery is because I would not allow myself to be corrected. I had to be right all the time! When wise people attempted—repeatedly—to reason with me and warn me (even to the point of yelling at me), I tuned them out. I would never be humble and listen. So, here I am, every time I'm in a large business meeting or at church, I'm humiliated because everyone knows how this woman treats me and just how miserable I am!

However, there is another possible scenario.

Acquaint yourself well with the strange woman, as described in Proverbs, and stay far from her when you encounter her in your environment. Instead, focus your attention on recognizing the woman God brings into your world. She will be someone that the older, mature women in your life will approve of. This is part of their assignment, so let them do it.

Then, once you are married to her (and not one moment sooner), you will take great erotic pleasure in your own wife, and as a result of your frequent sexual intimacy, children will be birthed and raised by this woman to love and honor you rather than being taught by the strange woman to despise you. In fact, they will be your spiritual offspring, uncontaminated by an ungodly alien influence in your house. This will give your children the greatest opportunity to be successful in business or prominent in government. This woman is affectionate and graceful, and God has given you His permission to enjoy a life of sexual pleasure with her, without always having to guard your back because your wife is guarding it for you.

If you could have this, why in the world would you allow yourself to be infatuated with a woman not of kingdom people or culture? Or engage in an illicit sexual relationship with a woman who is not your wife, or even someone that you are committed to marry?

Morally depraved men end up in a trap of their own construction.

We don't ponder this very often, but God observes the life of every man and weighs his intentions and attitudes (along with the resulting actions). Morally depraved men end up in a trap of their own construction. He is like the hunter who goes out into the forest and sets animal traps and forgets where he put them. The next week he goes to set more and ends up walking into a trap that he created. He then wonders why he's hanging upside down from a tree.

This is always the result of a willingness to engage in willful habitual sin. At the risk of sounding like a broken record, painful corrective discipline is the key to learning, either from your own pain or from someone else's. If children don't learn righteous discipline and character during their youth, the lack of it will destroy them as adults. In fact, I suggest that the rejection of corrective discipline often leads to unnecessarily risky behavior, that, if not corrected, can potentially lead to an early and untimely death. It is the difference between a "controlled burn" as opposed to a wildfire. A controlled burn is used by authorities to safely consume combustible material on the forest floor. In the end, the trees are a little scorched but protected from a small grass fire that could easily become a raging wildfire that could end up destroying the entire forest.

CHAPTER 14

RULE #10: AVOID THE EASY PATH

My son, if thou be surety for thy friend, if thou hast stricken thy hand with a stranger, Thou art snared with the words of thy mouth. Do this now, my son, and deliver thyself, when thou art come into the hand of thy friend; go humble thyself and make sure thy friend. Give not sleep to thine eyes, nor slumber to thine eyelids. Deliver thyself as a roe from the hand of the hunter, and as a bird from the hand of the fowler. Go to the ant, thou sluggard; consider her ways, and be wise: Which having no guide, overseer, or ruler, Provideth her meat in the summer, and gathereth her food in the harvest. How long wilt thou sleep, O sluggard? when wilt thou arise out of thy sleep? Yet a little sleep, a little slumber, a little folding of the hands to sleep: So shall thy poverty come as one that travelleth, and thy want as an armed man.
—PROVERBS 6:1-11

According to the October 16, 2018, issue of *The Balance* magazine, "In August 2018, US consumer debt rose 6.2 percent to $3.935 trillion." That's trillion with a T! Of this, "credit card debt totaled

$1.042 trillion, but credit card debt is only 26.5 percent of the total [US consumer] debt. It was 38 percent in 2008."

Consumer credit "card" debt is a relatively modern invention; however, according to Jeff Desjardins, in his online article "The History of Consumer Credit in One Giant Infographic," at VisualCapitalist.com, "It's actually been around for more than 5,000 years." From his infographic, I learned that the earliest archeological records are from ancient Sumerian agricultural loans dating from 3500 BC. In 50 BC, during the time of the Roman Republic, Cicero recorded his neighbor's purchase of 625 acres of land using credit. Modern installment payments for goods, was started by General Motors (GM) with the production of their first automobile in 1919. However, the "floodgates" were opened in 1950 with the advent of the Diners Club card. This was followed in 1958 by Bank Americard (later becoming VISA), MasterCharge (later becoming Mastercard), American Express, and Discover.

Of course, in the business world the use of credit, bank loans, and lines of credit are useful and sometimes even necessary in certain industries. Consumer credit, though, is not like this. It's based exclusively on the consumer's income, past payment history, and existing debt.

The word "debt" is derived from the Latin word *debitum* which means "contracted." *Webster's Dictionary 1828* defines debt as, "That which is due from one person to another, whether money, goods, or services; that which one person is bound to pay or perform to another."

At the end of Israel's 40-year odyssey in the Arabian Desert, they paused on the plains of Moab. While preparing to enter the land God had promised them a generation earlier, God declared to the nation a series of blessings that would come to pass for them. However, His promises were conditional, and their fulfillment was based on their willingness to cooperate with Him. As the creator of (literally) everything, God's constant desire is to see His people set apart to walk in dominion upon the earth; this includes our assets and our capability to increase them. It was there, that God made a remarkable declaration:

> And it shall come to pass, if thou shalt harken diligently to the voice
> of the LORD thy God, to observe and do all His commandments
> which I command thee this day, that the LORD thy God will set
> thee high above all the nations of the earth The LORD shall open
> unto thee His good treasure, the heaven to give the rain unto the
> land in his season, and to bless all the work of thine hand: and
> thou shalt lend unto many nations and thou shalt not borrow.
> —DEUTERONOMY 28:1

That's a mouthful. Let's unpack it.

At the beginning of Deuteronomy 28, God made a promise to the nation of Israel that had the potential to permanently shift the geo-political power structure of the earth. God desired to grant them dominion, not only as individuals, but as a nation. However, the condition on the promise was two-fold: 1) God required them to listen carefully to His voice, for them to completely obey it, and 2) They were to be utterly faithful to Him, absolutely refusing to serve the Babylonian deities proliferating in the gentile culture of that time.

God doesn't want automatons. He wants those He has chosen to agree with Him and accept His assignment for them.

Why were these conditions necessary? First, sin always brings a curse, and it is God's desire to bless those He calls His own. Second, God doesn't want automatons. He wants those He has chosen to agree with Him and accept His assignment for them.

God, at this time, did not prohibit the lending of resources within the Hebrew communities, but neither was it encouraged. If they did lend to each other, they were forbidden from charging interest. God wanted them to love and care for one another, like He did. Except for a major disaster (i.e. the loss of a breadwinner) God provided basically these two routes to prosperity. Again, listening to God and doing what He said. That is employing the wisdom of God and being faithful to Him personally—walking in relationship with Him and receiving His blessing. If you fast-forward to today, you can see how the descendants of this nation are still affected by promises of blessing.

According to Steve Sailer's article, "Jewish Wealth by the Numbers," in *Taki's Magazine*, "Jews are usually said to comprise about 0.2 percent of the world's population, so 11 percent of the world's billionaires means they're doing pretty well." The same article also stated, "Per capita, Jews are a little over 100 times more likely to become billionaires than the rest of the human race." This from the descendants of former slaves. Though most modern Jews are agnostics, as a people, they never forgot what God taught their ancestors about financial increase. Throughout their history, they never lost sight of the Law. They remembered the wisdom of God as it related to tithing or the strategies as related to the distribution of resources and multiplication of wealth.

With this tenth rule, Solomon continued to have a serious heart-to-heart discussion with his heir about all the ways for a king to lose his power, wealth, and/or influence. As the wealthiest man who ever lived, he reminded his son that it's one thing to gain wealth, power, and influence and another thing to keep it.

Solomon's wisdom (from which his wealth and power flowed) was born out of a prayer recorded in 1 Kings 3:5-14. In his humility, he recognized his need for wisdom and discernment in order to be a successful king. He didn't ask for wealth, fame, or conquest but for the ability to complete the assignment God had given him. Solomon's message here is, "There are no shortcuts!" The increase in our life, begins and ends with God. Solomon asked for discernment and got it. Nevertheless, as a bonus, God gave him wealth and power. However, Solomon understood that it was only by an abiding trust in his God and His principles that he would be able to keep it. In Proverbs 6, he discussed three ways to lose it: greed, laziness, and wickedness.

The first trap is greed. If an associate or colleague approaches you with a money-making idea that they want you to finance or guarantee, don't just agree to it (no matter how good it sounds!). Instead, be thorough in your "due diligence" of the project. If they are not close family members, at least conduct a thorough background check of the individual (in other words, do your research), get counsel from wise and knowledgeable business advisors, and most of all, pray and believe God for wisdom.

> Think before you speak, and do not obligate yourself without having done due diligence.

If you neglect to do these things and are seduced by greed, you have probably allowed your mouth to "write a check it can't cash." If you end up contractually obligated to your associate, and you realize that you cannot fulfill it, go to that person (with your attorney, if necessary), "humble yourself," and make every effort to escape this metaphorical trap. Run for your financial life, and realize that breaking contracts (even with a good attorney) can be very expensive.

Therefore, think before you speak, and do not obligate yourself without having done due diligence. And, if you do find yourself in a financial trap, do not wait another moment to get out of it. Allow these situations to be teaching moments, and remember not to make the same mistake twice. Make no mistake, the rush for easy riches can put you in a trap of great financial loss as taught by Solomon.

The next trap is laziness. Entitlement is a disease of the soul that afflicts both the rich and the poor. Entitlement is a perceived right to something which, in most cases, was not earned. The poor can feel entitled to certain government benefits like welfare (food stamps, TANF, etc.). The rich may feel just as entitled to the government subsidies and tax credits they receive.

Definitions.net defines laziness as "a disinclination to activity or exertion despite having the ability to do so." As an observer of the natural world and human behavior, Solomon directed his heir to the ant hill to carefully observe it. Apparently, the young man must have felt pretty entitled. I can hear him complain, "What! Me do manual labor. Not on your life!" Solomon as you could imagine, wasn't too impressed. "Get up, you lazy bum! Study the ant, and learn something!" The ant, Solomon observed, had no military leaders, no government bean counters, and no bureaucrats, yet they harvested and prepared food for consumption in the summer, and then they prepared more food in the fall to get them through the winter. It was as if Solomon were telling the young man, "How much longer are you going to lie there and do nothing, you entitled bum!"Good grief!

Then Solomon made a remarkable statement it Proverbs 6:10-11:

Yet a little sleep, a little slumber, a little folding of the hands to sleep: So shall
thy poverty come as one that travelleth, and thy want as an armed man.

He described here the path from wealth to poverty. It doesn't occur overnight but follows a certain pathology. This progression can occur in almost any form of destructive human behavior; however, this is applied to "The Pathway to Lack".

Step One

Your mind is deceived into thinking you don't have to work so hard. This seed, once planted in your mind, will continue to grow unless your mind is being renewed by the truth of God's Word, preventing the thought from gaining a foothold. At this stage, the enemy's goal is to get you to stop working or moving forward. This could also happen in someone's relationship with God, or their marriage, but for now we are dealing with things affecting our financial lives. This could be our business or career. At this point, the individual is still publicly and privately engaged and moving forward in life. This stage may or may not be noticed by the person experiencing it. Again, this can occur in a personal, professional, or even a devotional context.

Step Two

Your emotions begin to be impacted by the feeling of drowsiness. You now desire or long for a "break." At this point, the mental deception creates a false emotion. You are still publicly engaged, but privately you are beginning to check out and look for distractions. The emotions experienced at this stage can be anything from clinical depression to simple boredom. The distraction originates with an internal secret desire.

Step Three

Your will then starts making choices in line with your emotions. These choices have consequences that can cause one or more of the following things to occur.

You can become so disengaged from your job that you end up getting fired or quitting. If you are a business owner, your inability or unwillingness to focus your attention where it is necessary could cause your business to fail. Your marriage could also be affected as you may become so disengaged that you withdraw from your spouse and start looking elsewhere. This can lead to an emotional affair which, if not corrected, can lead to a sexual one.

Once you make the decision to disengage, no matter which method you choose, the result will be the same. Solomon used the metaphor of warfare, the description of the relentless devastating attacks of his father's mighty men, against his enemies. Once you disengage from your business or area of employment, destitution will "make war" against you, and impoverishment will come against you like a heavily armed champion fighter from the king's army.

Often, we hear stories of successful people making inexplicably foolish decisions, leading to financial ruin. They are, however, never snap decisions. They are the result of a gradual process. This again, follows the path of mental deception, false emotions, and then faulty or bad choices. Solomon revealed this process to his heir for him to see how to prevent or stop it.

The third trap is wickedness. During my childhood, my friends and I would, on occasion, get into mischief in the neighborhood. Of course, my mother understood that I knew better and would always ask why on earth I did it. My response was always, "Because Sam (or whatever his name was) did it." To this, my mother would invariably respond, "If Sam jumped off a cliff, would you?" My answer without exception was, "No, Mom, I wouldn't."

A wise man once said, "Show me your friends, and I'll show you your future." Why is that? Because as you mature into young adulthood, your peers' influence grows, and your parents' influence diminishes. This was probably a problem for Solomon as he described to his son the traits of evil men and the necessity of avoiding them. Solomon recognized (again) that sin brings a curse, and curses can result in financial loss. Let's examine the traits of these evil men.

These evil men, like Nimrod the first autocrat and enslaver of men, make it their aim to control your life, so they can take from you what it is that they desire.

» These men are intentionally DESTRUCTIVE. They are, however, fraudulent and two-faced, so it is not always immediately apparent. They can at least temporarily fool you with their perverse and deceptive speech.

» These men are ANGRY. They communicate malice with their facial expressions; their body language is both aggressive and disrespectful. For example, they point at you using angry, dramatic gestures instead of speaking calmly and peaceably. They also point with their feet when speaking to you, which in oriental cultures is considered a grievous insult.

» These men are DECEPTIVE. They are deceitful in both word and action. They silently scheme and devise evil, causing misery for others. They are a source of contention and instigate fights wherever they go.

Nevertheless, the massive weight of their own sin will eventually crush them. In a moment, in the blink of an eye, they will be mentally and emotionally destroyed without any chance of deliverance or cure. In other words, they could lose their sanity, end up with a very long prison sentence, or end up dead.

If you deconstruct this person, there are six qualities about him that God personally hates, and a seventh utterly disgusts Him!

1) ARROGANT COUNTENANCE

You have probably heard the saying about someone, "Looking down their nose at you." What they do is cock their head back and point their chin at you, forcing their eyes to look down toward their nose. Look up some old photographs of Benito Mussolini, and you will understand what "Il Duce" was communicating.

2) FRAUDULENT SPEECH

This stems from an unwillingness to submit to the truth. Arrogance and pride will often lead to a rejection of objective truth. After all, he may not agree with what God has to say; he would rather submit to his own version of the truth instead of God's. Therefore, if the mouth speaks what the heart is full of, the evil man will manifest itself in fraudulent speech.

3) DEADLY ABUSE of INNOCENTS

When arrogant and self-exalting men, who are unwilling to submit to the truth of God's Word, gain power, they do whatever they deem necessary to hang on to that power. The drug cartels are well known for their willingness to slaughter innocent people in their pursuit of power and what it will bring them. On a much larger scale, Josef Stalin was said to have murdered tens of millions of his own people in his naked pursuit of more power. It was British historian Lord John Acton, who was quoted in a letter to Bishop Creighton in 1887 that there should be one standard to judge all men. Why? Because, "Power tends to corrupt, and absolute power corrupts absolutely. Great men are almost always bad men, even when they exercise influence and not authority."

4) MEDITATIONS on EVIL

The "great men" mentioned before are men of the world who wield tremendous influence. When these men spend their energy meditating on wickedness, they create an environment for evil plots and schemes to flourish. It was while Hitler was imprisoned for treason against the Weimar Republic that he wrote, Mein Kampf (My Struggle), his autobiography and future plan to gain political power in Germany. This included a plan to eliminate the Jews which he blamed for the loss of World War I and Germany's economic problems following the war. This in turn led to the ascendance of the National Socialist Party—the Nazis—and the eventual murder of over six million Jews (and millions of others) who did not fit into Hitler's master-race narrative.

5) INTENTIONAL RUSH TOWARD EVIL

Those who spend their time meditating on evil will eventually find themselves moving toward it. You will always move in the direction of your focus! This is one reason Hitler and Stalin created youth organizations. They understood that if they could control what the youth heard, they would be able to control the narrative and replicate themselves in the youth. The evil man's focus is on doing evil and promoting personal gain through nefarious means. He will easily move in that direction, and because his conscience is seared and insensitive, it will not disturb him.

6) WILLINGNESS to GIVE FALSE TESTIMONY

This quality reflects that one is willing to lie in court and risk a perjury charge in order to get what he wants from others. This can be a politician, an organized crime boss, or a religious leader.

7) DIVIDER of RELATIONSHIPS

This is the quality God finds the most repulsive. I like to call this the "divide and conquer" strategy. This occurs when the evil man, desiring the trust and allegiance of people, will precipitate a crisis in the group. When the leadership is unable to provide a quick solution, the usurper (who created the problem in the first place) will step up and "solve" it. If the leader can solve the problem, the evil man may provide a compelling argument that the leadership is untrustworthy or incompetent. This will act to split the group, or by continued contention, force out the old leadership and install the new. This is often the anatomy of a church split or the potential destruction of a company or nonprofit.

This chapter explained three of the most common ways to lose wealth, power, and/or influence. They are carelessness caused by greed, aversion to hard work caused by a sense of entitlement (or simple laziness), and a willingness to use evil strategies to get what you desire only for it to destroy you in the end. Remember, there are no shortcuts to success; it's only by adherence to God's process of wisdom that we can increase our lives.

Remember, there are no shortcuts to success; it's only by adherence to God's process of wisdom that we can increase our lives.

CHAPTER 15

RULE #11: HOLD FAST YOUR PARENTS' INSTRUCTION

My son, keep thy father's commandment and forsake not the law of thy mother:

Bind them continually upon thine heart, and tie them about thy neck. When

thou goest it shall lead thee; when thou sleepest, it shall keep thee; and when

thou wakest, it shall talk with thee. For the commandment is a lamp; and

the law is light; and reproofs of instruction are the way of life: To keep thee

from the evil woman, from the flattery of the tongue of a strange woman.

—Proverbs 6:20-24

Today as most of us know, the family is under attack! From the hallowed halls of academia to the organs of the major news media and entertainment, the voice of postmodernism seeks to remove sexual boundaries, rewriting gender differences and roles. The instigators of these attacks have sought to feminize men, thereby stifling their ability to protect and provide structure to their families and especially their children. Consequently, women have been left with fewer marriage options, as young men seem less and less willing to accept the responsibilities of family life. This will serve only to reduce the cohesiveness of the family unit and degrade the moral strength young adults need to be successful in their personal and professional lives.

Solomon has always been identified throughout history as a man of legendary wealth. One estimate of his net worth is placed at approximately $2.2 trillion which gave the nation a per capita net worth of over $1 million! This lines up with the biblical description of the wealth that flooded the nation of Israel: "And the king made silver and gold at Jerusalem as plenteous as stones" (2 Chronicles 1:15). There was so much gold that it was considered common, and silver was what people commonly ate from. Unfortunately, the kingdom was divided soon after the death of Solomon, and so began the inexorable decline of the national wealth until Judah's final defeat by the Babylonian Empire in 598 BC. Again, it's one thing to obtain uncommon wealth and quite another thing to keep it.

In this eleventh rule, Solomon declared to his heir, "Observe [that is 'submit yourself to'] your father's commandments." The Hebrew word used is *mitzvah*, which are the restrictions in the Torah that God placed upon Israel, in order to make them His own. They also protected Israel from the curses caused by sin. However, he also said in Proverbs 1:8, "Forsake not the law of thy mother." In other words, "Don't cast off or desert the Torah taught to you by your mother from birth."

Connect the Bible's principles to your thoughts and emotions by making them a part of your daily meditations, thinking, and even your "self-talk."

So then, here we have the structural authority of the father and the principles of the Law as instilled by the mother. They are both required to raise happy, healthy, and successful children. The father is required because learning can only occur in an atmosphere of discipline, and discipline by its nature is painful. The mother is not equipped to provide this structure, as they can only go just so far by themselves. So your father provides the structure, and the law is taught to you by your mother. Nevertheless, you are responsible to keep them tied to your thoughts and feelings and make them part of your daily meditations.

Many of us (even most of us) because of family dysfunction, didn't learn success secrets from our parents. Nevertheless, everything required for a successful life is in the Bible, especially the Old Testament. Once you discover these principles, you must connect them to your thoughts and emotions, by making them a part of your daily meditations, thinking, and even your "self-talk." By reinforcing these thoughts and ideas, your mind will be renewed. Then, as you proceed through the journey of life, what your parents have passed on to you will govern your conduct as an adult. It will stand guard over your subconscious life so that even while you sleep, your thoughts will reflect what you meditate on while you are awake. When you wake up, these thoughts will speak to you. What you go to bed thinking about will be reinforced when you wake up. Therefore, it is important to make sure that what you go to bed with is from God.

In the beginning, God used the "one flesh" metaphor to describe the unity between a man and woman bound together in covenantal relationship, experiencing the depths of intimate physical oneness. Here, God uses a similar metaphor to describe what I call the "Singular Parental Unit." It is designed by God using another different type of integrated pattern. Solomon describes here a lamp and the light it produces.

The lamp of Solomon's era was composed of materials like clay, bronze, or even gold. It was normally oval-shaped with a reservoir on one end and a wick on the other. In any case, the material had to hold the oil and be lit to provide light. Solomon described the father's commandment, that is the restrictions or restraints, as something structured and functional. However, a completely functional lamp cannot give light unless it first contains oil and is lit.

The oil lamp wick, once lit, will give light, and the lamp's functionality will allow this. Just as the lamp and its structural integrity represents the father's protective authority and discipline, so does the light of the lamp represent the revelation of the Torah taught to the children from birth by their mother. All the basic concepts of the Torah are to be taught to the children by the mother as she is uniquely equipped to do this through her intuitive understanding of God's way and character; she provides the foundation for a life of godliness, wisdom, and dominion.

Solomon used this illustration to demonstrate the integration and functioning of a "Singular Parental Unit." In this context, two people are acting as one, in order to multiply themselves. The purpose for this, as it was in the beginning, was and is to pass on principles of dominion from parents to children. That is, dominion over their environment (business, social, legal, etc.) and over themselves. Until you have dominion over yourself, you will never possess the courage to stand up against the flood of temptation and moral opposition that is characteristic of the world system. However, if there is no father in the family, it will lack structural integrity, and without a mother, it will lack the light of wisdom and revelation. You must have both parents in the home to provide what I call the "painful chastisements" of disciplined instruction, which lead them to a flourishing prosperous life. Remember, all learning comes by pain either you own pain or someone else's.

Whenever discernment is discussed, the lesson of discerning counterfeit money is not far behind. The question commonly asked is, "How do you identify a fake $100 bill?" and the answer is, "By being very familiar with the true original currency." Solomon told his son specifically not to cast off or desert what his mother painstakingly taught him concerning the Torah (or the Law of God). Why? Because one of the images created in the mind of that young man from birth to adolescence, by his mother, was what a real woman walks, talks, and looks like thus, enabling him to accurately identify fakes. The fake in this case is a woman whose language is both flattering and arousing because what is in her is morally evil. Solomon here is again providing to his heir, strategies for keeping the power, influence, and wealth inherited from his father.

He then provided a warning, "Don't allow yourself to become infatuated by such a woman, don't allow yourself to become emotionally attached to her." Then he added, "Never allow yourself to be captivated by her fluttering eyelashes." So, what does that mean? In Eastern cultures, women's strict modesty standards over the ages have taught them to use subtle body language (in this case fluttering eyelashes) to signal romantic or sexual interest. So, why the dire warning? Because the price of sex with a prostitute is a "loaf of bread." In other words, it is a manageable cost. However, the strange woman, though married, will intentionally plan and scheme to position herself to sexually seduce and trap a young man, knowing that it could very well cost him his life. Solomon then asks a couple of gruesome rhetorical questions.

» Can a man heap flaming coals onto his lap and his clothes not be burned or catch fire?

» Can a man lay naked face down on glowing coals and his genitals not be blistered?

The answer to both questions, of course, is no! Nevertheless, this is the exact metaphorical description of what you would be doing if you had sexual intercourse with a married woman. ANYONE who is sexually intimate with her has violated her and would be considered guilty. In fact, it would be a matter of civil and divine law for both parties to be put to death. But, because the strange woman is an expert manipulator and possess a degree of power, she would throw her young lover under the bus in order to save her own skin.

Men (apparently) can more easily tolerate a thief that sneaks into their house to steal food over a man who commits adultery with their wife. If the thief is caught, they would pay restitution and then go home. However, the young man who commits adultery with a married woman is devoid of intelligence and lacks the awareness that doing it will destroy him. When the husband finds out, he will seek revenge upon the young man, and unlike the thief, the embittered husband will accept neither gift nor bribe, no matter how much it is. Moreover, even if the young man gets away with his sin, he may carry the scars of shame with him for the rest of his life, affecting the integrity of his own future marriage. It also opens a door of sexual perversion and dysfunction in the lives of his future children and grandchildren up to the fourth or fifth generation.

The lesson to be learned here is that parenting is a vital function. It cannot be adequately performed by just a mother, or a father, but requires both. Sometimes it is not possible because of circumstances beyond the control of either a single mother or father. Therefore, I am not condemning single parents but only saying that it was not what God had in mind, and it is not optimal. As a communicator of the wisdom of God, Solomon recognized this and painted a picture of the "Singular Parental Unit" and how it operates using the illustration of an oil lamp and how it produces light.

The lessons of functioning parents and the impact they have on their children is so important that it can shift the fortunes of generations of families and even nations. This makes it even more critical for those from godly functioning families to hold tenaciously to what they have been taught and to pass it on to their children, so they can pass it on to the generations that follow. It protects young men from sexual immorality and the curses that follow the young men and their offspring. Doing this requires parents who are willing to take the time, faithfulness, and energy to teach it. It also requires children to learn it and young adults to choose wisely to keep and protect it as they mature. In today's fatherless society, I would challenge the young men to find mentors and role models to hold them accountable before God to help them learn the critical disciplines of life set forth in this book.

I challenge young men to find mentors and role models to hold them accountable before God to help them learn the critical disciplines of life.

CHAPTER 16

RULE #12: AVOID "STRANGE" WOMEN

My son, keep my words, and lay up my commandments with thee. Keep my commandments, and live, and my law as the apple of thine eye. Bind them upon thy fingers, write them upon the table of thine heart. Say unto wisdom, Thou art my sister and call understanding thy kinswoman: That they may keep thee from the strange woman, from the stranger which flattereth with her words. For at the window of my house I looked through my casement, And beheld among the simple ones, I discerned among the youths, a young man void of understanding, Passing through the street near her corner; and went the way near her house.

—PROVERBS 7:1-8

Joseph's feet were swollen and painful from the long walk from the town of Dothan, where his father had sent him to check on his brother's well-being. He was still scraped and bleeding from his time in the pit his brother's threw him into. He could still see their hate-filled eyes as they mocked his pleas to spare his life. Reuben was the lone voice willing to save him from certain death, yet even he threw his lot in with the other brothers to sell him to the Ishmaelites. By now, the blood and sweat had turned the dust that covered him into a crust that he longed to remove.

The sun had long since departed, and the heat of the day was replaced by the cool and dark night. He longed to rest his weary body, but he dared not stop walking. Suddenly, his thoughts were interrupted by the commands of his Ishmaelite captors as the human cargo was directed to stop for the night. They were given water but no food, yet after traveling for days with little rest, he almost collapsed in exhaustion. He thought about his mother, Rachel, and his father, Jacob, before the exhaustion overcame him, and he was fast asleep.

He awoke suddenly to loud talking and activity where they had lodged for the night. It was then that he realized they were in a marketplace for the buying and selling of various goods to include the merchandising of human flesh. Without warning, one of his captives grabbed him by the arm and led him to a small crowd whom he discovered were interested in the human cargo for sale. Joseph felt himself flush with embarrassment as he was publicly examined, pinched, and probed like one of his father's livestock. There was a flurry of activity, yelling, more prodding, and more yelling until suddenly the crowd parted and an immaculately dressed Egyptian of authority and means gave the slavers the asking price and ordered his servant to collect the lad and take him to his estate.

The servant, in broken Hebrew, explained to Joseph that he was in Egypt and that his new master, Potiphar, was the captain of Pharaoh's guard. When they arrived at their destination, the servant helped Joseph to prepare himself for his new occupation. First, he had to scrub himself clean and remove the hair from his body. He exchanged the clothing of a Hebrew herdsman for the garment of an Egyptian slave. This consisted of a wig and a short linen kilt. His master, Potiphar, had him immediately put to work performing tasks in the maintenance of his household estate.

However, Joseph was not an ordinary slave. Aside from being a very handsome, well-formed, and attractive man, he was trained from his early youth to run his father's business enterprise. This involved such things as accounting, procurement, supply chain, and human resource management. What internally motivated Joseph's character, was *Yahweh*, the living God. This knowledge was passed on to him by his father who'd had a life-changing encounter with God himself. It was out of this deep reservoir of human experience that Jacob was able to impart, not only strength of character, but also a desire to know and obey his God.

Joseph was arguably history's most over-qualified employee, yet God had an assignment for him. He would have done well had he stayed at home and run his father's business. He may have even prospered during the famine (like his grandfather Isaac) and saved his family. Nevertheless, God's plan was not only for Joseph to save his family but also the population of the most powerful empire of his time!

Webster's Dictionary 1826, defines "favor" as "to regard with kindness; to support; to aid or have the disposition to aid, or to wish success to." Jacob favored Joseph as the only son of his love Rachel, and he poured everything into him. Not only did he impart his own experience into his favored son but also passed on to him the wisdom and knowledge of the oral tradition of his fathers before him. I'm sure this gave Joseph a great deal of confidence and his brothers a measure of jealousy and envy toward him.

You see, favor is not "fair," and it's not doled out equally, as some get more than others. Often, it comes to those who at least in our own minds, don't need it (or even deserve it)! However, favor almost always comes with an assignment, and God's assignments always bring opposition. That is a good reason to never desire another person's success. You have no idea what their assignment is, nor do you know what they have had to suffer. As such, God blessed and multiplied everything Joseph set his hand to, not for his own sake, but for the sake of the assignment because dominion always has a purpose.

Not much is known about Potiphar's wife; however, this much we do know: She was married to a person of great power and influence. She also was sexually attracted to Joseph and attempted vigorously to seduce him on many occasions.

We all know how the story ends. After ordering the staff to depart, she grabbed hold of the single linen slave garment and commanded him to ravish her. The average young male would have taken advantage of this situation but not Joseph. He feared and revered the God of his fathers and understood that God was the source of the favor on his life. He also displayed great loyalty to his master whom he refused to dishonor. This was someone who trusted and gave him access to everything that he owned, except for his wife.

When Potiphar got home and found his wife in possession of his favorite slave's garment, I don't believe her facts matched the narrative she tried to push. In fact, I'm convinced if he had believed Joseph indeed attempted to rape his wife, he would most assuredly have killed him on the spot without thinking twice about it. However, I believe he recognized his wife's intentions, and with the favor on Joseph's life, realized he could not put an innocent and righteous man to death. In his desire to prevent his wife's dishonor and scandalous behavior from damaging his own reputation, Potiphar had him locked up in jail for what turned out to be eight long years.

Joseph's life up to this point had been one of betrayal by his own half-brothers and then false imprisonment by someone he had served with excellence and loyalty. Nevertheless, it was not an attitude of bitterness that he carried with him to jail; he carried a reputation as a loyal, disciplined, and skilled administrator. It wasn't long before he was running the jail in which he was confined. The favor of God brought an impartation of wisdom and talent to Joseph, but while talent can activate dominion in your life, it takes a measure of character and personal holiness for you to keep it. This character can only come when it is exercised and then tested. Joseph's refusal to obey the ungodly command of his mistress and the ensuing imprisonment appeared at the time to be a crushing defeat when, in retrospect, it was probably his greatest victory! Eight years later, he was catapulted from the prison to the palace.

What were the keys to Joseph's successful escape from Potiphar's wife that set this series of events in motion? The words—the commandments and restrictions put on him by his parents during his childhood and adolescence—were. These simple concepts kept him safe from the strange woman, which in this case was Potiphar's wife, and they will keep you safe as well.

1) Decide ahead of time (before the situation occurs) to narrowly observe the rules and restrictions instituted by your parents during your youth.

2) By narrowly focusing on these principles, you will keep them at the forefront of your thinking. Being "narrow-minded" is not necessarily a bad thing as you always tend to move in the direction of your focus.

3) As you focus on these rules and restrictions, intentionally allow them to govern your thoughts.

4) Obey the resulting wisdom that God provides to you. This includes the same kind of advice about women that you would get from a wise female family member like a sister or an aunt.

The result will be that you will be protected from any woman (like Potiphar's wife) who sets her eyes upon you sexually or for any inappropriate reason.

What happens when these four principles don't help govern your life? Listen to Solomon's tale about a naive young man below and decide for yourself.

Being "narrow-minded" is not necessarily
a bad thing as you always tend to
move in the direction of your focus.

King Solomon was a ruler of staggering wealth, so it stands to reason that he didn't live in the "hood" but in the Beverly Hills or Palm Springs of his time as were the people he described. The king was an observer of people, and one day while leaning out of an open window, he saw a scene unfold. He noticed a group of adolescent males that apparently were silly, naive, and inadequately prepared to deal with the dangerous world they were born into. If not adequately trained to properly respond to the seductions of this world, they will almost certainly fall for them. The young men were also full of bravado. They bragged to each other about the size of the flocks and herds their fathers owned, the places they traveled with them on business, and girls and whom their parents had arranged for them to marry. But there was one young man, he noticed, who appeared distracted and restless who had slipped away from the group and walked across the street, avoiding the animals and the waste they left behind them.

Once this boy had crossed the busy thoroughfare, he walked a short distance on the other side before the king noticed him turning into a side street in his line of sight. This street was lined with the abodes of the merchants, who, thanks to the political alliances of the king, would travel to distant lands like Egypt, Nubia, and Syria with chests of gold and silver to purchase exotic tapestries, jewelry, and spices to sell in the marketplaces of Jerusalem. The young man then turned into what appeared to be a large flower garden full of blooming foliage where a bubbling spring watered everything. The woman of the house asked him to come by and help her with a "few things." Her husband, one of the many merchants in Jerusalem, was far away trading and conducting other business. She had asked him a couple of days before while he carried home heavy packages of grain for his mother. She seemed to be a cheerful and attractive woman his mother said actively helped the poor. She seemed to be modest in dress and temperament who fulfilled her temple vows and sacrifices. His thoughts went back to what the woman said to him at the marketplace. "When you arrive at the garden, sit down in the cool shade by the fountain, and I will be there shortly."

Upon his arrival, the side street in front of the garden was thronged with people returning from the marketplace. He had expected to be finished with his errand by now, and yet she still had not yet arrived. By this time, the sun was setting, and it was already dusk. The traffic on the once busy side street continued to lessen, until it had slowed to a trickle. The last of the merchants with their entourages of servants and guards were returning from their day's activities, weary but successful. The young man looked nervously at the dusky horizon and then at the few people hurriedly making their way along the street. The young man's face began to look anxious in apparent concern for his own safety. *The streets of Jerusalem become dangerous at night,* he thought.

Before long, the sun had gone below the horizon, and all that was left was a black night sky. A full moon began to rise in the eastern sky, casting a pale somber glow over the garden and the now empty side street. Suddenly, he heard steps behind him and turned in time to see a figure move out of the dark shadows. As the figure appeared in the moonlight, he saw, standing before him, the woman he was supposed to meet there much earlier. Rather than the modestly dressed woman of elegance, standing, and influence that he met earlier that week, there stood before him a beautiful woman dressed like the Egyptian women he had seen while traveling with his father. Her garments were of sheer, flowing fabric that hugged her form and shimmered in the moonlight. When he looked upon her, he was frozen in stunned amazement.

This woman had laid a simple, but well-planned and very effective, trap—a timeless trap that is still used to trap and seduce men today. The first part of the trap is based on deceiving the man. The woman seeks to gain the man's trust by portraying herself as a safe and trustworthy friend. Once she has gained your trust, she will ask to meet you somewhere that ordinarily you would be uncomfortable with. Nevertheless, like the young man we are discussing, you agree to it because you trust her, the location is within your comfort zone, and it appears to be a safe environment. Without your realizing it, she has gained a very advantageous position.

In Solomon's account, the strange woman probably instructed the young man to meet her in her garden just prior to twilight in the early evening. In his mind, it was not inappropriate to meet this prominent woman at that time and place. After enough time had passed when it was dark, and no one was around, she appeared. The strange woman (as you have probably gathered by now) only operates under the cover of deception and darkness. She revealed her true intentions here, only in the presence of her young object of desire, keeping her double life a secret.

As she moved further into the pale moonlight towards him, he became increasingly aware of her immodesty. When she finally stopped, she was inches away from him, the fragrance of spices caressing his sense of smell. In shock, his thoughts immediately went back to the last time he saw her. She was graceful and elegant but also modest. She was known for her generous giving at the synagogue and her many sacrifices at the temple. She gave him the impression of being a proper and upstanding woman, faithful and duty-bound to her husband, a successful and influential merchant in the city of Jerusalem.

The woman, sensing his uncertainty and fearing he would leave, suddenly grabbed him and gave him a passionate, lingering kiss. After she released him from her grasp, the look on her face was not soft but hard, and her voice was commanding, "I have just given a thank offering, a promise which I have fulfilled today. I eagerly escaped to encounter you, to diligently look for you, and I have finally gotten my hands on you."

The account doesn't provide the woman's age; however, she knew what she wanted and would perform any scheme necessary to obtain it. Behind the mask, she was rebellious, dramatic, and unwilling to be productive and care for her household. She spent her time scheming how she could trap and seduce men. By sexually arousing him by sight and touch, she was able to lead him where she wanted him to go and do what she wanted him to do.

In *Webster's Dictionary 1828*, the word "impudent" is defined as "shameless; wanting [lacking] modesty." However, the Hebrew word used could also be translated as "strong" or "hard." There was nothing in her countenance expressing anything warm or sweet. She sarcastically declared that she had just left the temple. In fact, she was in such a hurry to encounter the object of her desire that there was no mention of her having eaten it yet, as was the law. This encounter was premeditated by this woman who diligently searched for this teenager to trap him.

And she continued:

I have covered my bed with exquisite embroidered tapestries with figures having the appearance of carvings, upon the finest Egyptian linen. I have sprinkled my bedroom with crushed myrrh, aloe, and cinnamon to perfume it. So, come with me, and let's abundantly satisfy ourselves with sexual passion until the dawn and enjoy ourselves with lovemaking. You see, the master of the house is not at home but has departed on a long

remote journey; he has taken a bag of silver with him and will return at
the time he has set.

The descriptions of the lady's room not only reveal the woman's access to wealth but also her level of preparation. My guess is the "carved images" on the tapestries were exotic and beautiful pagan images, which though, forbidden by God, were desired by her anyway. Her bedchamber may have been a private room where she slept and indulged herself with secret affairs. The myrrh, aloeswood, and cinnamon used to perfume her bedroom were most likely compounded into an intoxicating fragrance.

This woman's well-planned trap was now being baited. The second step of the trap was (and is) to arouse the man in body and mind while at the same time assuring him. She did this in three ways.

1) The woman aroused him by sight as she was dressed in revealing clothing ... then by smell with an intoxicating fragrance ... hen by touch, by grabbing him and giving him a passionate lingering kiss. She aroused his mind by describing to him how she prepared everything for him and with her description of what they would spend the night doing.

2) The woman used the fulfillment of a religious obligation as a means to communicate her religious observance to prevent him from seeing her religious indifference while maintaining a dysfunctional trust in her.

3) The woman then removed the possibility of any consequence from the equation by assuring him that her husband was gone and would not be back for a couple of weeks.

What happened next? Her abundant captivating coaxing caused him to compromise his moral standards, and by the smoothness of her language, she misled him. He followed behind her without hesitation, as a cow is led to the slaughterhouse, or as an imprudent fool to the discipline of leg irons. Until the blade of a knife or projectile has pierced his liver, in the same way a bird is promptly trapped, he doesn't realize that his life has ended.

I can imagine Solomon saying, "Hear me right now, you sons, and obey the word I am speaking to you. Don't allow your emotions to turn you aside to her lifestyle. Don't wander away on her well-worn paths. For she has overwhelmed many whom she has wounded, many powerful men were destroyed or even killed by her. Her house is the pathway to hell descending to the bedroom of destruction."

So then, let's review what happened here and what the young man could have done differently to avoid the strange woman's trap.

» **She met him alone in a private place.**

Unless the woman you are planning to meet for the first time is an immediate family member, it would probably be a good idea to meet her in a very public place.

» **She met him under the cover of darkness.**

A wise person once told a young man, "Always be home by 11 pm. Nothing good happens when you are out later than that." When someone (man or woman) wants to trap you, they will almost always wait for the cover of darkness which is why most crimes are committed at night. If you are married, you should refrain from being alone at night with any woman who is not a family member. If you are single, you should not be out late alone with any woman in any private place.

» **She dressed in an intentionally and overtly sexual manner.**

By insisting on the requirements above (meeting publicly and in broad daylight), most women will be deterred from dressing inappropriately. If a woman wants to meet you alone, at night in a very private place, you need to decline that invitation. However, if you take these precautions and she shows up dressed inappropriately in the daylight and in public, you must have the courage to tactfully and politely excuse yourself from a potentially compromising situation.

» **She grabbed him and kissed him.**

Never allow a woman who is not your wife or fiancé (or family member) into your intimate space when you are alone. According to cultural anthropologist Edward T. Hall, "intimate space" is within 6-18 inches of your body.

» **She made a perverted and hypocritical connection between her religious devotion and her desire for the young man.**

Be careful of women who use their religious devotion as a way to gain your trust and build a romantic connection with you. You don't need to live in suspicion; however, you do need to walk in discernment. If she is married, maintain your distance, both physically and emotionally. If she is single, find out if she is under spiritual authority and accountability. If she is not, rebellion against your God and His requirements may not be far away; maintain your physical and emotional distance. If any woman would try to use her devotion to gain a sexual connection, run away from her as fast as you can. She is obviously trouble!

» **She shared very personal details of her private sexual life.**

The woman described her bed to the young man and how she prepared it and her bedroom for sexual activity. This type of conversation is a big "red flag" and should be immediately cut off as soon as it is recognized.

» **She gave an impassioned invitation for all-night sex.**

By the time you get to this stage, she is very confident you will say "yes." Of course, if you haven't ended the discourse by the time you get to this point, you probably won't at all.

Sexual seduction is a process which you have the choice to end at any stage, but the longer you wait to act, the harder it will be to say "no" and walk away. The fact is, you may not want to walk away, but if that is the case, you need to keep this in mind. Even if you get away with it and avoid being assaulted and stabbed or shot and killed by a jealous husband (which is always a distinct possibility), illicit sexual activity carries with it a curse. Do you want to be responsible for a future legacy of promiscuous children, grandchildren, and great-grandchildren? If not, then you must guard and protect your emotions, and don't allow yourself to become infatuated with one of these women. Every man that she encounters in this way she destroys. Solomon calls the strange woman's bedroom a "chamber of death [or ruin]." We can be certain that God is not interested in ruining our fun but is protecting us from a life of misery.

> We can be certain that God is not interested in ruining our fun but is protecting us from a life of misery.

As children, we often received lessons from our parents about character and the type of people we associate with. As we matured into adolescence, those lessons became more and more important to our futures. By adulthood, if we remembered the things we learned from our parents, and actually did them, chances are we made wise choices in whom we married. If not, then we probably ended up in a less than desirable relationship that failed. The strange woman in Solomon's account actually ruined two lives. She made her husband miserable and endangered the life of the young man, quite possibly causing his death. Remember the lessons of your parents, or you may end up in either one of these unenviable positions. Remember that the strange woman never gives—but only and always takes.

CHAPTER 17

BONUS RULE: CHOOSE YOUR WIFE WISELY

Who can find a virtuous woman? for her price is far above rubies.

—PROVERBS 31:10

Much of the second section has focused on the dangers and pitfalls of the strange (or adulterous) woman. She is the spiritual progeny of Semiramis who, according to the Jewish historian of antiquity Josephus, was the mother (and later the wife) of the first global despot Nimrod. The last part of this section will focus on her antitype, the "virtuous woman." The Hebrew word chayil translated "virtuous" also means powerful or capable. This describes a woman of dominion and authority, who walks in the original assignment of the first woman to aid and protect her husband. Much of what we know about the Proverbs 31 woman is narrowly focused on preconceived ideas of what a godly woman is supposed to be and act like. In this chapter, I hope to provide additional insight and shed more light on this remarkable woman of ability and talent. It should also be noted that while Proverbs 31 was entirely recorded by King Lemuel, the information itself was provided by his mother who appears to be herself a virtuous woman.

Though my father provided a framework of discipline in our household during my childhood (I always considered him the "enforcer"), it was my sharp-tongued English mum who taught me the lessons of life as I navigated the minefield of childhood and early adolescence. I feared the physical strength and imposing stature of my father, but I respected the voice and piercing glare of my mother!

As a youth, I would propose that Prince Lemuel was beginning to take on the qualities of a young womanizer until his mother the queen decided that she'd had enough. So, she sat him down and discussed with him three things that he would never forget.

Lemuel's mother began her discourse, by giving her a son a piece of her mind: "What in the world are you doing, son? You who are heir to the throne. Remember, it was I who gave birth to you! I gave you to God when you were born, so you belong to Him." The words of a mother haven't changed much in 2,500 years. So, when your mother brings correction to you about something you should not be doing anyway, remember King Lemuel's mother and the three big things she taught him.

1) Be very careful with your interactions and social intercourse with women, and chose your relationships with the opposite sex wisely.

During the last chapter, we discussed at length about the strange woman and the necessity to avoid any entanglements with her. King Lemuel's mother sought to protect her son from this usurper and destroyer of men whose goal it is to take the power and authority of the king and appropriate it for herself (both then and now). You must also never allow yourself to be seduced into giving up your inheritance to one of these women.

2) Never become intoxicated with alcohol (or any other substance).
In Proverbs 20:1, Solomon issued a strong warning about alcohol consumption, which Lemuel's mother wholeheartedly agreed with:

Wine is a mocker, strong drink is raging: and

whosoever is deceived thereby is not wise.

Rather than asking, "Can I do this and still go to heaven?" the questions
I should ask are these: "Is it wise? What is the wise thing for kings to do?"
I can almost hear his mother saying, "Your friends can do those things,
but you may not!" and her reasoning was quite compelling.

» The substances could intoxicate the king and cause him to misrepresent
God's judgment. All law ultimately flows from a divine source as kings
are held to a higher standard. Kings are carriers of the royal DNA, who
were born to carry the authority to perform the assignment given to
them by God. They were born to exercise the dominion of the kingdom.
Today, these are the regenerated ones of this age, those who are born
of God. They are then filled, energized, and transformed by Him until
they become just like Him. The judgment of the king must never be
perverted because justice must be rendered on behalf of those unable
to obtain it on their own. Those who are captive to sin are the ones who
consume substances (like alcohol) to soothe their pain and misery of
mind and body. They consume intoxicating substances to forget their
poverty and sadness—even if it's only numbing temporarily.

» Intoxicating substances prevent the king from operating on behalf
of others. King Lemuel's mother told him, "Speak for those who are
unable to speak for themselves, and argue for those unable to represent themselves." These are adolescents who have survived loss or
abandonment. They have no one and are orphans, both physically

and emotionally. These are often survivors of absentee parents who divorced so that one of them is no longer in a relationship with the child, or the child is suffering the permanent loss of the parents by death. Lemuel's mother also encouraged her son to be a voice of justice of those depressed in mind or circumstances, those considered financially and/or emotionally destitute. A king's duty (whether he be secular or spiritual) is to use his power and authority to bring order where it is lacking and not merely to serve himself. He is to speak for those who have no voice, those who are caught in the prison of generational poverty and misery. The king, moreover, doesn't leave them there but uses his wisdom and knowledge to show them the way out.

3) **Be intentional in setting standards for your future spouse and stick to them. Don't compromise the future of your posterity by settling for less than God's potential best for you.**

When broaching this thought, if you will allow me to paraphrase, the mother asked her son a remarkable question:

"Who can acquire a wife of character, power, and means?

For the value of her assets far exceeds precious gems."

Lemuel's mother wanted her son to think, to question his assumptions about women and look beyond mere beauty or sexual attraction. The question she asked was, "What does a prospective wife bring to the table?" His mother understood the desire of the strange woman, and she was protecting her son from usurpers who would covet his wealth, power, and influence. The virtuous woman on the other hand, would not only possess assets of her own but would also be a woman of character and internal strength—a strong woman capable of multiplying the young king's assets and not consuming them.

Lemuel's mother continued:

> *"Her husband completely trusts in her with his whole heart*
> *so that he will have no lack of profit. She will cherish him*
> *well and not be wicked to him as long as she lives."*

His mother understood well and desired for him to also see that the foundation of any relationship, especially marriage, was trust. In the last chapter, we saw both the wickedness and unfaithfulness of the strange woman. I believe it was her untrustworthy character that not only explains her marital infidelity but also the inordinate financial demands placed on her husband, requiring his extensive travel to distant lands to feed her persistent appetite for imported luxury goods. Here, however, King Lemuel's mother describes to her son a woman who is not only trusted to be faithful in marriage but who can also be trusted to wisely handle his assets, to be a producer and not simply a consumer. This woman was seen as a safe harbor and a refuge to her husband. When life brought forth its challenges, she would be a source of solace and comfort. She was gracious, kind, and loving, and the atmosphere she creates in the home is one of peace, prosperity, and love for as long as she lives.

> *"She diligently searches for wool yarn and linen fiber, and uses her*
> *hands to produce something valuable. She is like the merchants' ships;*
> *she leaves and brings back fruit and grain from distant places."*

This woman understands that to make a business successful, she must find quality materials and produce a product that will sell for a profit. So, she diligently searches for the appropriate materials. As the astute businesswoman that she is, she would much rather spend her money purchasing quality fiber and yarn than using her valuable skill and time making it herself. As a skilled craftsman with access to other skilled people, she understood the impact of quality materials on a finished product. Once she obtained the materials, she worked with passionate joy to create things of value. This woman of means and character, with the resources at her disposal could just as easily have hired out all the labor. Nevertheless, she kept part of it for herself to do because she took pleasure in her work.

She was not only a craftsman with an eye for business, but she cared for the needs of her entire household. Lemuel's mother metaphorically referred to her as "merchants' ships" as she would not delegate her grocery shopping to an estate manager, or a chief of staff, but would do it herself. In fact, she would even travel great distances herself, to ensure the proper quality and quantity of goods.

"She arises from her sleep when it is still night, and serves prepared food to her household, and a defined amount of provision to her servant girls. She proposed to herself the idea of obtaining a parcel of land, and then bought it. After working hard to prepare the ground, she planted a vineyard."

This woman NEVER hit the snooze button on her alarm clock, and she NEVER slept in! She consistently, day in and day out, woke up before dawn to care for her family and staff. This woman of means and authority could have easily delegated this duty to her staff, but her character would not allow it. She not only cared for the dietary needs of her family, but she also cared for the needs of her young servant girls. No one lacked provision or proper care in her household.

This woman NEVER hit the snooze button on her alarm clock, and she NEVER slept in!

An effective time manager, she also made time to evaluate and perform her due diligence on a parcel of land she sought to acquire. She apparently understood the potential uses for the land and what would bring the highest return on investment (ROI); she determined the best use for the land would be to plant a vineyard. Then she purchased the land, and hired the people required to plant and tend the vines to raise grapes in order to produce an excellent wine.

"She puts on strength, power, and might like a belt, and increases the power of her forearm. She perceives that the profit from her sales will be bountiful, so her candle burns well into the night."

This woman of character and authority made a choice every day to be powerful, strong, and bold. The metaphor of "girding" or "putting on" strength, speaks to the daily choices to work hard as opposed to the strange woman of the last chapter who lived in idle luxury with no drive or productivity. Of her, Solomon remarked in Proverbs 7:11, "She is loud and stubborn: her feet abide not in her house." Unlike the virtuous woman, she is like a spoiled child; she is petulant, rebellious, and lacks restraint. She has no interest in the responsibilities of her household but in the short-term satisfaction of her own personal lusts. This caused her to make poor decisions that were destructive to both her short- and long-term interests and those she was intimately involved with.

As the choices made by the virtuous woman aligned with her purpose, she was able to discern the results of her decisions before she made them. She knew intuitively what she needed to do for her business revenues to keep increasing and was willing to keep on working after everyone else had gone to bed.

"She reaches forth with her hand to grab the spindle and
her other hand holds the distaff steady. She reaches out to
and embraces those depressed in mind or circumstance,
and reaches out with her hand to rescue the destitute."

This remarkable woman understood how things were efficiently produced, by using refined materials, to produce products that will eventually be sold in the marketplace. On the other hand, she was also able to produce her own linen thread or wool yarn. I don't believe this was based on need, but rather on her desire to maintain proficiency of a skill learned at a tender age, that may have been passed on to her young servant girls. In the ancient art of spinning thread or yarn, a distaff was held in a woman's left hand. It was a wooden rod that held the fibers and kept them from tangling. In her right hand, she held a spindle, which held the twisted fibers. She would simply twist the fibers with her left hand, from the distaff of fibers in her left arm, and wrap it on the spindle she held in her right hand.

The next thing displayed is her compassion, which is expressed in two ways:

1) She reached out to the downtrodden and depressed.

She had compassion on people who had lost hope. You see, poverty is not simply a "cash-flow problem." It is primarily mental and emotional. She not only gave people things like food and covering but became to them a broker of hope! When people have thrown in the towel on life, it takes a virtuous woman to make the necessary deposits into their lives to bring them back into the mainstream of society again.

2) She reached out to rescue the destitute.

This harkens back to Proverbs 31:9, where Lemuel's mother had told him to "plead the cause of the poor and needy." These were the materially destitute: the widows who had lost the financial support of their husbands through death and orphans who lost one or both parents through death or abandonment. She utilized her substantial resources to provide aid to these people and her influence to encourage others to do the same. This queen set the bar high for those coming behind her. This to prove that queens are not indifferent and self-absorbed but hardworking and compassionate.

"She does not hesitate to produce white for her household, for her entire household is clothed in scarlet. She fashions her own bed coverings; her apparel is of the highest quality linen and purple."

This woman's household was never concerned about cold weather because they were always adequately clothed! However, I don't believe they were referring to actual snow falling from the sky but to the snow-white color of linen and the labor-intensive effort required to convert the linen thread to cloth. Then, there was even more labor required to obtain the organic material from the *Coccus ilicis* which is the scientific name for the scarlet worm. This provided the scarlet coloring for the fabric; however, the tedious, time-consuming process is what produced the scarlet fabric. As a result, everyone in her household was well-clothed, including the servants.

The bed coverings in her bedroom were not imported from Egypt, as we recall from our account of the strange woman, but were produced by her own hands. These were linen coverlets, beautifully and intricately decorated. The clothing she wore was not just linen but a superior grade with the feel and texture of silk. However, to set her even farther apart as a queen, her luxurious fabric was dyed purple, the color of royalty! This color was derived from the extracted gland of a rare Mediterranean shellfish *Bolinus brandaris*.

"Her husband is famous in the gates of the city, where he sits in judgment with the governing body of the land. She manufactures and sells fine linen undergarments; and delivers leather belts to the Canaanite merchants."

During King Lemuel's time, the cities were built with protective walls. The openings that allowed the people in and out of the city were protected by large wooden or metal gates that were closed at night or during attack. It was here that the king held court and the government operated, making it a place of power and influence. This king was able to govern successfully and walk in great power and influence because his wife ran his household diligently. As it turned out, it was the virtue and excellence of the queen that propelled her husband the king.

This woman, again, was not a consumer, but rather a producer, indicated by yet another income-stream producing enterprise. Today we put cotton sheets on our beds to sleep on; however, during that time, you wore the "sheets" on your body in the form of a linen tunic. This woman produced and sold these items in the marketplace. However, the leather belts that she also produced were of the highest quality and were sold to Canaanite merchant seamen who sold them everywhere they went.

"Power and majesty are her garments; she will rejoice at the future.
Her speech gives vent to wisdom, and imbedded in her language
is the precept of piety toward God and kindness to men."

Her speech released what was in her heart, where there resided a rich source of wisdom.

The queen's power was reflected in the boldness of her decision-making! This was not a weak or "mousy" woman, nor was she a rebellious or bossy type. She was a woman who had the trust of her husband. While he was fulfilling his purpose and function as a ruler in his area of dominion, she was engaging in one business enterprise after the other, exercising dominion in her area of gifting and competence. Though she did not sit at the city gate like her husband, the king, she was nevertheless an influencer—her majesty and beauty, not originating with her outer and corporeal appearance, but with her inner strength and character.

Her speech released what was in her heart, where there resided a rich source of wisdom. She spoke life to those around her by expressing joy and optimism about the future, which I believe gave her continuous entrance into the lives of others to bring life and then transformation. These could have only taken place when expressed through her heart of kindness and mercy.

> *"She accurately observes the future procession of her household, and does not consume food of laziness. Her sons mature and become successful, leave her feeling blessed; her husband also, and he boasts loudly about her."*

As an observer of the caravan of life, this woman was able to able to peer into the distant future of her children's lives. This discernment allowed her to determine each child's gifting and their resulting future potential. In other words, she paid careful attention to her children's development; in doing so, she was able to deeply impact their lives. Doing this required her constant engagement with them on every level. This would not have been possible for an indolent, lethargic woman who would simply not have had the energy that it would have required. As her children matured, especially her sons, the influence and care of their mother created an environment conducive to their future success. When it came time for them to leave their mother to start their own families, they were able to leave in joy and peace and carry with them a legacy to pass on to their own children. Their rejoicing was probably also heard by their neighbors and friends. Her husband apparently did something similar by boasting loudly, by raving and celebrating her. Since he was seated at a place of power and influence, everyone going in and out of the city must have known just how wonderful that she was!

> *"An exceeding number of young maidens have achieved beauty and strength, but you have exceeded them all. Graciousness is a sham and a sparkling appearance is empty, but a woman with a*

reverential fear of the Self-Existent One, she shall be made to shine

by being loudly celebrated. Grant her the reward of her labor, and

let her business accomplishments be celebrated in the city gate."

This exclamation was probably made by King Lemuel's father in a load boast on behalf of his wife. During this time, there was probably no shortage of beautiful and charming women in Israel. An exceeding number of them were accomplished and able, but Lemuel's mother had apparently continued to grow and increase until she had outshined them all. Then Lemuel's father probably made one of the most remarkable declarations in all of Scripture, echoed by his son, "Favor is deceitful and beauty is vain; but a woman that feareth the LORD, she shall be praised" (Proverbs 31:30).

The word translated "favor" is derived from the Hebrew word *chen* meaning "graciousness." The verb tense is *chanan* meaning to "bend or stoop in kindness to an inferior." Favor or graciousness in this context is an admirable quality, so why would the king appear to minimize it? Because when exercised outside of the character of God, especially when combined with captivating physical beauty, it could be a formidable means to bend and manipulate men to accomplish her will. If graciousness does not originate from a desire to express the heart of God in service, then there is probably an ulterior motive, and if that is the case, it is not a pure motive. However, as this woman did have a reverential fear of God, she was loudly celebrated. She could be trusted by both her husband and her God!

As a result of her husband's trust, he was enjoined to, "Grant her the reward of her area of dominion," which in this case was entrepreneurship and business. He continued, "And let the products she produces cause her to be recognized and celebrated in the place of power and influence." King Lemuel was a wise king who was well taught by his mother. By allowing her to excel in her area of dominion and celebrating her publicly, his father caused his mother to be a positive reflection of himself. This made him even more influential and increased his own leadership visibility among government and marketplace leaders, both local and distant. This was a lesson of great value to the young prince who would soon be king. The virtuous woman, like his mother, is the example of the type of woman every man needs. Because of her wisdom, King Lemuel knew to avoid the strange woman, for she only takes. The focus of her life is to covet, and her desire is to usurp.

THE ENEMY OF KINGS AND THE KINGDOM

CHAPTER 18

LOVE NOT THE WORLD

Love not the world, neither the things that are in the world. If
any man love the world, the love of the Father is not in him. For
all that is in the world, the lust of the flesh, the lust of the eyes,
and the pride of life, is not of the Father, but is of the world.
—1 JOHN 2:15

n the later part of the 1st century (approximately 90 AD), the venerable apostle John, the disciple whom Jesus loved, wrote a letter to a group of fellow believers. His desire was for them to remain true to the pure gospel of his Master and Lord. In doing so, he made a remarkable commanding statement, "Love not the world." As a young Christian, I was constantly admonished about "the world," and why I shouldn't do "worldly things." I usually succeeded in avoiding these things, but as a look back on my life, I realize that my focus may have been too narrow. The world, as I had been taught, was this nebulous idea that if my unsaved friends did something, then I probably shouldn't do it. Things like drugs and alcohol were obvious to me, but I struggled with things like dances and movies. These questions never got satisfactory answers, and as I look back, I realize that I was asking the wrong questions. The question I should have asked was not, "What can I do?" but, "Where can I live?" or, "What culture do I belong to?" The world had been turned into a religious code of things that I was allowed and NOT allowed to do. Whereas, the "world" in Greek, kosmos, was a political, religious, and cultural system created by Nimrod.

In Genesis 10:8-9, it was said of Nimrod, "He began to be a mighty one on the earth. . . . He was a mighty hunter before the LORD." This means two things:

1) He dissolved any covenant he had with God in order to set himself up as a tyrannical king—the first in history.

2) His lust for power drove him to ruthlessly murder his opponents. Those who refused to bend to his will were eliminated.

Nimrod was insolent before God and had contempt for Him. His entire political, religious, and cultural order was built on fear created by threats and intimidation. Out of this, came the institution of slavery, which was not only the buying and selling of flesh, but also included what I call "willful bondage." This is a transaction that at least, on the surface, is of great benefit to the employee. They may be promised substantial compensation and even celebrity; however, the terms of the contract may make them little more than slaves to their employer. Nimrod created this slavish antichrist system at Babel, where he was worshiped as a god—as the first Baal. This system survived, however, even after God confused the people's language and the people were scattered.

Archeologists and anthropologists have discovered similarities in the architectural layout of ancient cities and societal norms of their occupants. Pyramid-shaped structures have been discovered not only in Egypt but also in Central America and China. Baalistic human sacrifices, according to "25 Cultures That Practiced Human Sacrifice," an article by Owen Jarus in *Live Science*, occurred in almost every civilization of the ancient world and were almost always perpetrated on children or adult slaves. This antichrist system of Nimrod continues to modern times.

So then, why shouldn't believers in Christ prize this Baalistic world system? Stupid question, right? Well, not really because apparently believers in Christ get trapped and pulled in, or John would have never issued the warning. There are two different systems on the earth according to the Bible: the world and the kingdom of God. The first was founded by Nimrod, and the second was founded by *Yeshua* when He came to earth with each system governed by its own set of values.

The world, that is, the Baalistic system according to John, is governed by three primary values:

1) The "Lust of the Flesh" or the longing for forbidden and unrestrained animal sexual cravings.

Sexual cravings that are not restrained but acted upon become a source of bondage and a means and method to control and enslave. After sin was introduced to humanity, the first emotion they experienced was shame. It was originally said of the first man and woman, that they were "naked and not ashamed." Having complete emotional freedom, they walked with God, and this they did withease and transparency. Nevertheless, it is sexual sin that brings such suffocating shame—especially sex acts involving the same sex or underaged youth. These can bring so much shame that they become a means for the powerful in politics, media, entertainment, and business to control, by threatening the public release of damning images of them in the most humiliating, or even criminal, sexual situations. The lie pushed in the beginning, however, is that unrestrained sex without boundaries will bring fulfillment. This is the deception of pornography; it makes promises that it can never keep, neither for the entertainer, nor the entertained; neither the seducers, nor the seduced. The lie fools everyone—no one gets a pass.

2) The "Lust of the Eyes," or the materialist craving for stuff usually for its own sake.

This usually includes a bigger and better house, a nicer, newer car, and clothes with only the trendiest brands. Like the lust of the flesh, the lust of the eyes is not restricted by economic class. I have seen the latest trends in clothing, electronics, and automobiles in almost every economic class. Why? Because if you are not in the kingdom of God, you are by default, a part of the antichrist world system with a value system opposed to the kingdom that you belong to. God told the Israelites not to covet (Exodus 20:17) because when one lusts after something—anything—they can buy it if they have the money. If there is no money to buy it, you can borrow the money and go into debt (financial bondage) for it. If the lust is strong enough, and there is no money, there is always the option to steal it and pay for it with your freedom in the form of a jail sentence.

3) The "Pride of Life" or the vain and arrogant swagger for your present means of livelihood.

This goes beyond sexual hedonism or materialism to the root of all sin— which is independence from the Creator. It is the mindset of I don't need God to care for me, nor do I want Him dictating my life. This again is not dictated by economics or by social standing, as it was first established by Adam in the garden of Eden and codified by Nimrod into his political and religious systems. This arrogant independence can be found in those individuals who think they can do it their own way without God and governments that exclude God and His Word from public and civic discourse.

Why did Nimrod think it was it so necessary to eliminate the Creator from the society he ruled? As a destroyer and enslaver of mankind, Nimrod was at his core a bitterly angry covenant breaker. As the grandson of Ham, he had heard the oral account of the cataclysm and the ark from his grandfather, and what the earth was like when he came out of the ark. He continued the story, explaining how after they had begun to establish their lives after the floodwaters receded, his great-grandfather Noah planted a vineyard and made wine with the resulting harvest of grapes. After overindulging in his brew one day, Noah ended up inebriated and naked in his tent.

Scripture doesn't say he was unconscious but suggests that he was incapacitated. Thus, when Ham showed up, Noah was aware of it. Some theologians believe Ham had in some way defiled his father. Others, such as R. J. Rushdoony, in his "Genesis: Volume 1" of *Commentaries on the Pentateuch*, point to Ham's contempt for his father and the authority he possessed. He may have even spoken to his father in a contemptible manner, so when Noah recovered from his drunken state, he remembered. Noah's reason for cursing Canaan instead of Ham was first of all because of God's previous blessing on Noah and his sons (Genesis 9:1), which could not be revoked by man (Numbers 23:20). It was also because the sin of the fathers can adversely affect their descendants (Deuteronomy 5:9). I also believe this curse planted a seed of bitterness in Ham. This bitterness brought forth rebellion in Cush, and then open warfare from Nimrod. This first *ba'al* (leader) was the original anti-Christ, and the world system he formed was the one spoken of by the apostle John.

We then fast-forward to a young man traveling from Ur to an unknown place in the ancient region we know today as Palestine. He had surely heard the tradition told and retold by the elders in his family of the great Creator and Judge. However, it was not until after God spoke and revealed himself to him that Abraham became the father of a nation—one whose purpose was to stand in opposition to the world system created earlier by Nimrod.

As previously mentioned, Abraham's grandson Jacob went down to Egypt with his household to escape the effects of a famine. They were given the best of the land in Goshen until a Pharaoh (probably a foreign king) ascended the throne, not knowing how they had delivered the empire. He then enslaved the nation of Israel, forcing them into hard labor, making bricks and constructing extensive building projects during his reign.

However, instead of destroying them, as Satan desired (Exodus 1:15-22), God strengthened them and caused the women to give birth to physically robust children. With a very low infant mortality rate, the population of the nation Israel continued to increase until the land of Goshen overflowed with them. Healthy children at birth grew into healthy adults, creating a nation free of the health issues that plagued the Egyptians. This ensured the Israelites' ability to make the arduous journey through the Arabian Desert and into the Promised Land.

> *And it came to pass, that at midnight the LORD smote all the firstborn*
> *in the land of Egypt . . . and the children of Israel did according*
> *to the word of Moses; and they borrowed of the Egyptians jewels*
> *of silver and jewels of gold and raiment: And the LORD gave the*
> *people favor in the sight of the Egyptians, so that they lent unto*
> *them such things as they required, and they spoiled the Egyptians.*
> —EXODUS 12:29, 35-36

When God began to deliver the nation out of Egyptian bondage, he judged both Egypt and the world system that empowered them. On the final plague of these judgments, while still in Egypt, God gave the nation their first instructions. These words dealt first with deliverance from judgment and then deliverance from bondage.

Deliverance from judgment occurred during the final plague when God went through the land of Egypt to kill every first born of the Egyptians, whether human or animal (Exodus 12:12). The only things that would separate those who were judged by God and those who were delivered were God's instruction and their obedience to it. The nation Israel was commanded to slaughter a lamb and use hyssop to paint splotches of the lamb's blood on the door lintel overhead and both door posts on either side. This instruction went out from Moses to the Israelites, but God is no respecter of persons. The judgment of *Yahweh* fell upon every household without lamb's blood on its doorway whether Israelite or Egyptian. This was a foreshadowing of *Yeshua* shedding His blood as the Lamb of God, to protect us from the judgment coming upon the world, which though we are all in it, we are not all of it.

Deliverance from the bondage occurred after they personally plundered the Egyptian population and walked out on them. If then, the blood satisfied God's judgment, then the stripping or plundering of the Egyptian population provided the Israelites, a destitute nation of slaves, with a staggering amount of personal wealth. We will discuss the purpose of the wealth after we unpack why God insisted the Israelites leave Egypt in order to worship Him in the first place.

First, God wanted the Israelites to be freed from the Baalistic system of slavery and false religion in Egypt. Second, God wanted to break the government-imposed system of dependence that held them in economic bondage. *Yahweh* wanted their trust to be in Him and Him alone. Now, when they left the mighty Egyptian Empire, *Yahweh* provided their food and water supernaturally and made sure their clothes and shoes never wore out.

Obviously, there were no markets in the Arabian Desert to spend money, so why would God command the Israelites to strip the wealth from the Egyptian population? There are four possible reasons for this:

1) The Egyptian Empire had stolen the labor of the nation Israel, and Yahweh always requires that the thief return seven times more than he took. (see Proverbs 6:30-31)

2) As slaves to the Egyptians, Israel owned almost nothing, and it was only as they were able to obtain wealth, that they would no longer be dependent on the system. They would possess sufficient resources to preclude being dependent on others and allow them to form future sources of capital.

3) Some of what they took were weapons to fight with when they encountered enemies along the way (like the Amalekites).

4) They were able to acquire the resources to establish their own governmental and spiritual relationship structure that stood in opposition to the world system. This started when God called Moses to the top of Mount Sinai and gave him what we now call the Ten Commandments.

The Ten Commandments were a massive paradigm shift for the Israelites.

And God spake all these words, saying, I am the LORD thy God which
have brought thee out of the land of Egypt, out of the houses of bondage.
—EXODUS 20:1-2

The Ten Commandments were a massive paradigm shift for the Israelites. As it was, they were freed from the bondage of slavery, but the world system they left no longer provided for them or gave their lives structure. God had to provide that structure Himself; thus, these commandments were the foundation of a new culture of divine authority and leadership for the children of Israel.

They were no longer at the mercy of a Nimrodic government that robbed them of their freedom and their labor and a false religious system that defiled their minds and their bodies. They would once again experience dominion over their environment, the forces of darkness, and themselves. Self-rule under God's authority became possible once again, but the concept of personal responsibility had become foreign to them. Hence, the painful process of mental and emotional transformation had begun.

The very first statement God made was of self-identification. He stated, "I am the LORD (*Yahweh*) thy God." Next, God made it clear that He and no one else had delivered them out of the bondage they were in. They had been slaves for generations, and all they knew was what they saw around themselves in Egypt every day.

> *Thou shalt have no other gods before me.*
>
> —EXODUS 20:3

As no one else on earth would have been able to successfully confront the crown jewel of the world system and the greatest military machine of that time, God wanted to make it clear to Israel that it was He and He alone who crushed the false gods of Egypt. Therefore, *Yahweh* emphatically insisted they bring no other gods into His presence as no other being in the heavens or on earth is remotely worthy of His exalted position!

Idolatry is part and parcel of the great river of religious history dating back to the ruthless domination of Nimrod. Egypt, in fact, was one of the earliest descendants of this most ancient Babylonian system and was saturated with idolatry. As slaves to the Egyptian system, they spent many generations marinating in that idolatrous culture which God had to get out of them. As His new "bride," God was jealous and was not willing to share her with any potential "suitors." Therefore, it was necessary for God to purge them of their old mindsets and get Egypt out of them. If God did not do that, they would certainly end up in bondage again to the world system they had just been delivered from. God simply desired an intimate relationship with the Israelites, but to gain that he had to supplant the false Babylonian religious thought of Egypt with the truth of who He was.

Another aspect of this prohibition was God's original ordained order. Prior to the fall, God put mankind in the place of dominion over "the fish of the sea, over the cattle, and over every creeping thing that creepeth upon the earth" (Genesis 1:26). Therefore, the worship of these creatures is not only a slap in the face of the Creator but a defilement of man who was created as the representative image of the living God.

> *Thou shalt not make unto thee any graven image.*
> —Exodus 20:4

While the second commandment forbids the formation of images, it also prohibits them from being worshiped. Why? Because God (and Satan) fully understand the requirements of His covenant and the penalty for breaking it (Leviticus 26:14-39). The result is a cause-and-effect progression:

1) Once a person willfully engages in the worship of Ba'al and his cohort (in one of their many forms), a door is opened in their life allowing a spirit to bring them into immediate bondage to serve and labor for it.

2) Idolatry always results in sin especially sexual sin and debauchery. At first, it's exciting and pleasurable, but it always comes at a terrible price.

3) Sin then brings a curse, and curses result in judgment (Numbers 25:1-9).

This judgment unfortunately follows family bloodlines from father to son to grandson to great-grandson and then on to the ancestor who revealed his distain of *Yahweh*, based on the choices he made to sin against Him. On the other hand, he grants favor to the multitudes of those who affectionately love Him and observe His *mitzvah* (the order and restrictions placed on them). This revealed to the nations by the mark God put on them that they were His own. Every man that I have ever met desires an exclusive relationship with his wife and would never tolerate a woman in his life who desired to share her affections and sexual intimacy with other men. May I suggest that we feel this way because being made in God's "likeness" includes how He expresses His love. Therefore, His expression of emotional and romantic passion would follow the same path.

Thou shalt not take the name of the LORD thy God in vain.

—EXODUS 20:7

This commandment follows the injunction against idolatry because the false gods of the Babylonians (and then the Egyptians) required them to do terrible things in the name of their gods, including sexual orgies and even human sacrifices! *Yahweh* was (and is) absolutely repulsed by this. Moreover, today, one of the objections of the unbelieving world to the gospel of Jesus Christ is the terrible things that people do in His name. God forbids this in the strongest terms as His name and reputation are at stake. So then, be very careful how you walk and speak. Don't ever violate or smear God's character by doing or promoting evil or engaging in falsehood and connecting His name to it.

Remember the sabbath day to keep it holy.

—EXODUS 20:8

The fourth commandment contains a declaration by God that He created the heavenly bodies, the atmosphere, the earth, and everything in it in six days. Then on the seventh day, *Elohim* "rested." It is absurd to imagine that the almighty God gets tired. In Psalms 121:4, the psalmist declares, "Behold, He that keepeth Israel shall neither slumber nor sleep." In other words, He doesn't get drowsy, nor does He allow himself to lose consciousness or awareness by sleeping. Nevertheless, He stopped and took a step back to admire His creation, everything He had just made. He then commanded the people to imitate Him and do the same. He wanted them, on one day a week, to stop and view everything through the lens of a beautifully innovative and creative God.

The secondary purpose of a sabbath is to allow our physical bodies to rest and recharge. Again the *mitzvah* (commandment) was and is never based on legalism but upon separation from the world system. The Israelites did not belong to it, and how they lived would reflect that truth. Created originally as representative images of *Elohim*, God merely desired for the Israelites (and us today) to walk this out as people that were to be like Him with His passions, desires, and priorities.

Honor thy father and thy mother: that thy days may be long

upon the land which the LORD thy God giveth thee.

—EXODUS 20:12

The Arabian Desert, where these commandments were given, was intended merely as a detour around what may have been certain defeat by a superior, well-trained military force. Though it ended up being a 40-year detour, at the completion of the journey, they entered a beautiful, fertile, and well-watered land with natural springs and rain in its season. They lived in houses they didn't build and ate from trees they didn't plant. However, what good is wealth or increase, if you are unable to hang onto it? Without character, you will never keep what it is you have gained.

However, what good is wealth or increase, if you are unable to hang onto it? Without character, you will never keep what it is you have gained.

So then, how do you obtain the capability to keep what you have been given? It doesn't "take a village." It takes fathers and mothers. What is the secret to releasing these resources? It only takes one thing, and that is to honor your parents! A great deal of generational success will flow out of this because if you honor, you will submit. If you submit, you will listen. If you listen, you will be teachable. If you are teachable, you will learn what you need to be successful. It all starts with how you treat your parents, so honor them. The promise for expressing that honor was a long life in the land which the supreme God delivered to them. How you treat your parents will determine what you learn from them. This would include strategies for growing in character, improving health, and gaining (and keeping) material wealth. These will affect the length and quality of our lives, so be sure to honor your parents!

> *. . . Thou shalt not [murder].*
> —EXODUS 20:13

"Sin is a terrible thing," said Mary McDonough. "It is the dethronement of God!" However, the act of murder takes it a step further as the murderer then occupies the position of God. The first time the penalty for murder is mentioned in the Bible is in Genesis 9:6:

> *Whoso sheddeth man's blood, by man shall his blood*
> *be shed: for in the image of God made He man.*

In the beginning, as we recall, God Himself formed man as a perfect, exquisite clay figure and breathed "spirit life" into him. This life not only made him a self-conscious being but God-conscious as well. He was God's own representative upon the earth to govern this physical realm. Thus, first, murdering a human being is a destruction of the image of the living God. Second, murder often destroys unformed lives—people for whom God had a purpose and destiny that will never see it fulfilled. Finally, it damages the lives of the people left behind—mothers, fathers, and children—in the wake of the tragedy.

Thou shalt not commit adultery.
—Exodus 20:14

Sexual intimacy outside of the marriage covenant is dangerous on an emotional, psychological, and physical level. The primary purpose of sexual intimacy was established after God formed the woman and brought her to the man to cement a unity of soul. This in effect, "welds" them together into one united entity. This "one flesh" construct is then appropriately equipped to establish a household, raise children, and prepare them for adulthood and beyond. While murder ends the life of an individual, adultery's destruction is just as serious and far-reaching.

When a man or woman engage in an adulterous relationship, they:

» Separate themselves from God in order to escape the conviction of sin.

» Stop communicating with their spouses out of guilt.

» Argue with and denigrate their spouses to provide a mental justification for the faulty emotional choices they are making.

» Lose the ability to effectively parent their children.

» Risk a divorce with the ensuing financial devastation to the family when they are discovered by their partners. They even risk acts of violence being perpetrated against each other, up to and including murder of one or the other spouse.

In the end, you have an emotionally and financially devastated single parent raising emotionally wounded and damaged children. All of which would have been avoided by simple obedience.

Thou shalt not steal.
—Exodus 20:15

One of the hallmarks of family is loyalty and fidelity; however, the foundation of these is trust. This was a necessary component of a society whose dwellings were tents which had no locks (as was also the case of the permanent dwellings in the Promised Land). The sovereign God was forming a society based on the rule of law where imperfect people could be taught to obey the law of a perfect God and in doing so live in internal peace. This, on the other hand, draws a stark contrast between the characters of God and mankind's enemy, Satan.

God is and always will be a giver. He is the giver of life, joy, peace, freedom, provision, and everything else we need (and even some of what we want!). Satan, on the other hand, comes to kill and steal and destroy. It's almost as if God said, "You carry My image and you represent Me, so don't act like your enemy. I am going to teach you to be a giver like Me, and you will receive the blessing from it." Also, in order to promote societal cohesion, it was necessary to vigorously protect the loyalty that can only come through trust because the greater the trust, the greater the intimacy, and the greater the strength of the nation of Israel, both socially and militarily.

> *Thou shalt not bear false witness against thy neighbor.*
> —Exodus 20:16

The Nimrodic civil system of Egypt was both capricious and brutal. The justice system was not at all like the system created by God requiring witnesses before accusations of crimes are made. In Egypt at that time, if you were accused of a crime, you were guilty until you could prove your innocence. Just ask Joseph. He was jailed upon the false accusation of one woman. If Pharaoh had not experienced his disturbing dream and called for Joseph to interpret it, he may well have died there!

Nevertheless, *Yahweh* is a God of justice and requires it because it is in His character and part of who He is. So, through Moses, God created an entire legal system based on the rule of law that everyone under it, whether great or small, would be required to provide truthful and impartial testimony to prove guilt of a crime. This is the foundation of our modern Western judicial system. However, giving a false testimony (also called "perjury") endangered God's system of justice that He'd started to implement. This top-level injunction against perjury would preserve the integrity of the justice system and prevent the falsely accused from being unjustly punished.

> *Thou shalt not covet . . . anything that is thy neighbor's.*
> —EXODUS 20:17

Finally, the tenth commandment is what I call the "catch-all commandment," or actually the "foundation" commandment, depending on your perspective. In the beginning, after God created mankind, He walked with them in perfect intimacy. There was only one law, and it was related to accepting or rejecting "the assignment." After the first couple rejected the assignment and elected to live independent of God, sin entered the river of humanity and with it covetousness. The Hebrew word for "covet" is *chamad*, which actually means "to delight in." This is not such a bad thing unless the thing you are delighting in belongs to someone else. That can be a problem. I believe God mentioned this commandment last because at its core, it is at the root of every other sin.

If I don't like God's rules, I find another God to "delight in."

If I don't like the wife I have, and I "delight in" yours, then I try to take her.

If you have money that I would "delight in," I murder you and take it.

Coveting is a terrible thing! It is a mistrust of God and His goodness. Rather than elevate mankind, it reduces God to the level of men. *Yahweh* is the supreme, living God. Everything He does toward us is for our loving care. These ten commandments declared to men by God were the foundational boundaries placed upon a chosen group of people to distinguish and separate them out of the great river of humanity. Every other law, prophecy, psalm, or word of wisdom is based on these foundational commandments. The Torah (the Law), as set forth in the first five books, was created by God to demonstrate His protective love for us and to mark us as His own.

CHAPTER 19

THE KINGDOM ESTABLISHED

For unto us a child is born, unto us a son is given: and the government

shall be upon his shoulder: and his name shall be called Wonderful,

Counsellor, The mighty God, The Everlasting Father, The Prince of

Peace. Of the increase of his government and peace there shall be no

end, upon the throne of David, and upon his kingdom, to order it,

and to establish it with judgment and with justice from henceforth

even for ever. The zeal of the Lord of hosts will perform this.

—Isaiah 9:6-7

Immediately following Adam's sin, God declared a curse upon the serpent that was two-fold: 1) The appearance of the serpent was changed from one of beauty, elegance, and gracefulness to being reduced to slithering on the ground without arms or legs, and 2) It would, at some future time, be judged and crushed down by the descendent of the woman whom he deceived. Not only would a man crush it, but He would crush its governmental power and legal authority as well.

The first part of the curse occurred immediately when Lucifer was stripped of his heavenly beauty and forced instead to slither in the dust. Nevertheless, until the "new man" *Yeshua* showed up on the scene, Lucifer would still have the capability to deceive mankind into building his kingdom. This kingdom found its greatest expression through Nimrod—history's first one-world government with an anti-christ ruler. However, it was always God's desire to have a people of His own. So, from the patriarchs to Moses and then the kings, men of God foretold a Messiah, a great champion who would not only deliver man from a Nimrodic antichrist government and false religion, but from his own sin, depression, and demonic prison.

The remarkable prophecy from Isaiah 9:6-7 describes a man, who, unlike the first Adam, accepted the assignment to crush the rebellious forces of darkness. The prophecy begins by describing a man-child who would also possess God-like characteristics. This son of the nation Israel was the messianic champion described in Genesis 3:14-15. He was destined to rule a world empire, shouldering the responsibility for it Himself. His rule would be a perfect one, unfettered by the baggage of the current Babylonian system. His authority and character, as represented by His Name, were destined to be proclaimed across the face of the entire earth.

What is He?

A marvel and a miracle.

What does He do?

He is a problem-solver.

He is a powerful warrior-king.

He is the perpetual LORD of health, prosperity, and peace.

One of His names is *El-Gibbor*, which is translated in English as "mighty God." It is a compound word that can also be rendered "Warrior-God," describing a champion, a valiant hero who is fully God and fully man, the One whom God prophesied of to the serpent in the garden. The prophet Isaiah described one whose honor, authority, and character as represented by His name would be proclaimed over the face of the earth. Thanks to modern telecommunications and media, *Yeshua's* name has and continues to be proclaimed around the world.

Thanks to modern telecommunications and media, Yeshua's name has and continues to be proclaimed around the world.

Isaiah 9:6 described Messiah's kingdom as one of health, prosperity, and peace. As the future king, He will have abolished death, poverty, and war. His government will not be a democracy; there will be no Constitution or Bill of Rights. It will be a universal monarchy, based on the rule of the King, in a world at peace. There will be no militaries, no police, no crime, no hospitals, and no cemeteries! This will be a universal empire without limit that will cover the face of the earth. *Yeshua* will rule as Messiah from the throne of David, the name of the warrior-king anointed by the prophet Samuel whose name also means "love." The place of His dominion will be over the face of the entire earth, and He will dominate the nations. In the process, He will create a perfect judicial system based on divine law which He will enforce through His own perfect character.

God, it was said, would fulfill this by the strength of His own passion as God of the angel armies.

Of course, God understood in the strength of His own wisdom, that before Messiah's kingdom could be manifested in power, glory, and dominion, it first had to be established in the collective heart of mankind. Before men and women could operate in dominion and fulfill their original God-given mandate, *Yeshua* as deliverer had to accomplish a change in them first.

> *The spirit of the LORD is upon me; because the LORD hath anointed me to preach good tidings unto the meek; He hath sent me to bind up the broken hearted, to proclaim liberty to the captives, and the opening of the prison to them that are bound; to proclaim the acceptable year of the LORD.*
>
> *—Isaiah 61:1*

Though the purpose of God for mankind has always been dominion, the fall brought this purpose to a screeching halt! Man had not only been broken beyond repair but was bound in a prison of his own creation. What was God's solution? *Yeshua*—the mighty warrior-God of Isaiah 9:6—had to first come to the earth as the life-giving liberator of Isaiah 61:1, the One on whom the Holy Spirit would rest. Contrary to many of our concepts of Him, *Yeshua* was not a religious figure but a governmental one. These prophecies bear no resemblance to the portrayals of *Yeshua* throughout history that are pathetically feminine. These prophetic words describe someone of great power and authority who was to pay the price of our sin in order for us to have a relationship desired by God.

What would be the purpose of this anointing which was reserved for kings and priests? It would bring good, cheerful news to the humiliated and beaten down race of Adam. It would bind the wounds of those who are emotionally damaged, liberate those caught in the clutches of sin, and open the prisons to free those held in chains by the forces of darkness.

Before Messiah could come to the earth to establish His earthly kingdom in glory and power, He would have to first come to earth to establish His kingdom in the hearts of the people. Though God had revealed Himself and displayed His great power to mankind throughout history, it would ultimately be necessary for Him to come as a human being to the planet He created to clean up the mess made by the first Adam. When it was the right time, *Yeshua* would announce the arrival of the "Kingdom of God." This would not be "a" kingdom but "the" kingdom, ruled by Messiah and not mere men.

Once He made the announcement, He then demonstrated His power and authority by:

» " bind(ing) up the brokenhearted"

The earth is full of emotionally damaged people. Multitudes have been shipwrecked by rejection, bitterness, and emotional trauma. God desires for us to be like Him with nothing broken or missing—accepted, joyful, and whole. Only whole people can walk in dominion.

» " proclaim(ing) liberty to the captives"

Sin has captured us all. Messiah's mandate was to bring freedom from a natural proclivity to sin that was passed on to us from the first Adam. This pathway to transformation occurs step-by-step. The more of God's life that flows into us, the more of His character we possess, and the freer we become. Only people who are freed from sin walk in dominion.

» " and the opening of the prison to them that are bound"

A host of people across the face of the earth are demonized. The spectrum of demonization can go from minor influence to complete control. People on both ends of the spectrum require deliverance which only His coming would bring. Only those who walk in freedom from demonic bondage can walk in dominion.

» " to proclaim the acceptable year of the Lord"

The Messiah would arrive on the scene, announcing to the sons of Abraham, a new era of reconciliation between God and man, to include a new government . . . a new kingdom . . . ruled by the King!

Who was this king, this God-man, and when would He be revealed in history?

> ## For His people to operate in dominion, He had to do something transformational in them first.

In the fourth chapter of the Gospel of Luke, there is an account of Yeshua's introduction to the world. After thirty years of obscurity, He was handed the scroll of the prophet Isaiah to read. He went straight to 61:1 and read it out loud and declared Himself as its fulfillment. Then, for the next three years, He proceeded to do exactly what we just discussed. Everything *Yeshua* did was pursuant to the singular purpose of establishing His kingdom in people. He accomplished this by first healing their emotions, setting them free from the drive to sin, and delivering them from demonic bondage. This also included miraculous signs and wonders like:

» Turning water into wine.

» Feeding five thousand men and their families with a few fish and a couple small loaves of bread.

» Healing the sick and the infirm.

» Bringing dead people back to life.

Yet, His primary mandate was still Isaiah 61:1.

For His people to operate in dominion, He had to do something transformational in them first. This included teaching them the value system and culture of the new kingdom that He was establishing upon the earth.

In the previous chapter we discussed what the apostle John identified as three aspects of culture of the Nimrod world system. Now, I want to take some time to discuss what the Messiah, who was prophesied to come, taught about the value system of the kingdom He came to earth to establish. During His Sermon on the Mount at the beginning of Matthew 5, Jesus taught nine Principles of Kingdom Culture. In biblical numerology, nine is the number of completeness and finality. These principles lay a complete foundation for everything else *Yeshua* taught and are the foundation stones of kingdom culture.

1) "Blessed are the poor in spirit. . . ."

Being "poor in spirit" describes a powerlessness or helplessness of the "rational spirit" which involves the ability to think, feel, or choose. Whereas man's natural or fallen nature is one of independence from God, being "poor in spirit" is a willingness to be voluntarily dependent on God. This is not passivity, which is ceasing to think. It is a profound recognition of our own human limitations and the ability to discern what we do and do not control.

Possessing the kingdom of heaven is the exercising of dominion which is possessing sovereignty over yourself, your environment, and the forces of darkness in conflict with you. This can only occur from a position of absolute dependence on God.

The worst thing about the fall was that mankind was no longer dependent on God for everything they needed but depended upon themselves. Instead of walking in intimacy with Him "in the cool of the day," they now had to accomplish everything, "by the sweat of their brow." Rather than working together with God in a coordinated effort to exercise judgment over Lucifer and the forces of darkness, they were deceived into acting independently of their Maker. They abdicated their royal position and became slaves of the one they were created to judge.

The first foundation stone of Messiah's kingdom culture is
DEPENDENCE, the first mile marker on the road to dominion.

2) "Blessed are they that mourn. . . ."

To mourn is to lament over one's sin; it is to feel a passionate distress over the condition of our souls. As we experience sorrow and grieve over our wretched condition, God causes us to see His goodness, which then leads us to repentance. It is only after receiving a revelation of the darkness of our own sin that we can, by contrast, experience so vividly the brilliant light of Christ. It was this revelation that caused the apostle John to declare:

> *This then is the message which we have heard of Him, and*
> *declare unto you, that God is light, and in Him is no darkness*
> *at all. If we say that we have fellowship with Him, and walk*
> *in darkness, and do not the truth: But if we walk in the light,*
> *as He is in the light, we have fellowship with one another, and*
> *the blood of Jesus Christ his son cleanseth us from all sin.*
>
> —1 JOHN 1:5-7

When we mourn, that is, when we lament and grieve over our sin, God doesn't leave us in our misery but consoles and strengthens us; God's way is not condemnation but transformation.

> *The second foundation stone of Messiah's kingdom*
> *culture is SORROW FOR SIN, the second mile*
> *marker on the road to dominion.*

3) "Blessed are the meek. . . ."

Notice here what Yeshua did not say WEAK. According to Vine's Expository Dictionary, the Greek word for meek, praus, denotes gentleness. It is the same word Yeshua used in Matthew 11:29 to describe Himself when He said:

> *Take my yoke upon you, and learn of me; for I am meek and*
> *lowly in heart: and ye shall find rest unto your souls.*

This describes a person of strength and competence, someone confident enough to not express it unnecessarily. However, neither is meekness an excuse for cowardice in the face of evil, as even Yeshua expressed His physical strength when He made a scourge out of rope and drove the corrupt merchants and money changers out of the temple (John 2:13-15). Even in the face of evil, it requires wisdom to know when to and when not to fight.

Those who walk in meekness are promised an inheritance from God just as the Israelites, after crossing the Jordan River, were given land by inheritance. They lived in houses they didn't build and ate from trees they didn't plant. In the same way, the meek shall be rewarded for their gentleness. They will, by their wisdom and self-control, receive a portion of the kingdom in their area or gifting and competence, like the Israelites who received their portion in Canaan. The Greek word translated "earth" is the word ge. The gentle, as they continue to walk in God's strength over their own, receive more kingdom real estate as God considers them more trustworthy with what He gives them. They are not attracted to the world system but to the land God has promised them.

A good example of this was the different choices made by Abraham and Lot. When given a choice by Abraham, Lot chose the land of Sodom, a metropolis on the well-watered Jordanian plain. Sodom was not only steeped in the Babylonian world system, with its false religion and corrupt culture, but it represented man's pride and self-sufficiency. Abraham traveled in the opposite direction of his nephew, and his humility in that situation allowed God to bring him into his inheritance.

When we display meekness in situations where it would simply be easier to exercise our own power, God leads us on the path to our inheritance. Remember, dominion always depends on God's power, not our own.

The third foundation stone of MEEKNESS avoids the exercise of our strength over God's, the third mile marker on the road to dominion.

4) "Blessed are they which do hunger and thirst after righteousness. . . ."

The "hunger and thirst" here is actually an "ardent craving and desperate thirst." This is an accurate description of Yeshua's physical state after His wilderness temptation. After forty days and nights in the desert without food, He was profoundly hungry. In fact, his body was in a state of starvation, and He never forgot the desperate hunger He experienced! After five and a half weeks without food, your body is weak and has difficulty performing the most mundane tasks.

When your inner man experiences such a desperate desire for food and drink (and I'm not talking about a Big Mac and a Coke), only that which God can provide, He will fill you with it.

The desperate pursuit of the righteous sterling character of Christ is described as "hunger and thirst" because it requires:

» The nourishment of the Word.
» The water of the Word.

When you make the Word of God your food, it teaches you to walk in your identity as a son while giving you the wisdom of a father. Desperately hungry people can only be satisfied by food that can fill them that is the solid meat of the Word. On the other hand, when the water of the Word is consumed, it slakes your thirst but also possesses a higher purpose. Like physical water that cleanses and renews your internal organs and blood, the water of the Word cleanses and renews your inner man. In your pursuit of the sterling character of Christ, you must desire the bread AND the water of the Word. Only those who seek Him like this will God promise to fulfill and satisfy.

There is no dominion without a holy, sterling character, and there is no character without a desperate HUNGER and THIRST for the Word. The fourth foundation stone is a desire for HOLINESS, the fourth mile marker on the road to dominion.

When you make the Word of God your food, it teaches you to walk in your identity as a son while giving you the wisdom of a father.

5) "Blessed are the merciful. . . ."

Yeshua was mentioned in the gospels at least five times as either "having compassion" or "being moved by compassion." It was His compassion that caused Him to miraculously feed five thousand men (and their families) and raise a young man from the dead. The English word "merciful" is translated from the Greek adjective eleemon meaning "actively compassionate." Yeshua, as the last Adam, was compassionate because it was His nature to be so. In fact, may I suggest that it would be impossible for Him to be anything else.

Normally, mercy is meted out by people who don't think they need it themselves, but magnanimity is not based on compassion. In the kingdom, where the Law of Sowing and Reaping is in effect, those who sow mercy, will reap a harvest of "active compassion" in their own lives. Just as our expression of generosity to others will bring generosity back to us, so will those who are merciful to those around them bring the same active compassion upon themselves—not from God but from people.

The fifth foundation stone is MERCY (or active compassion). This fifth mile marker is not only the path of dominion but the proof of dominion.

6) "Blessed are the pure in heart. . . ."

Though God created the first couple for dominion, they elected to follow a different path. The original assignment God placed in their life was ruined, and their purpose was frustrated. In the beginning of creation, it was said of Adam that he "walked with God." He lived daily in the presence of God, who I believe revealed Himself as a breath or wind, the ruwach. In the seventh generation from Adam, Enoch was born. Possessing a righteous character enabled him to walk in the continuous presence of the living God and experience the ruwach the same way Adam did in the garden! Though Enoch was conceived in sin like all of Adam's other descendants, his heart was purified by continuous cleansing. In Job 1:5, it was said of Job that he offered continual burnt offerings, which I believe he may have learned from Enoch's example.

The Greek word for "pure" in Matthew 5:8 is katharos, the origin of the English word "catharsis." It indicates "purification through purging or cleansing." Those who walk in purity of soul by continually confessing their sin to God and living a life of repentance will live in an unfettered and unclouded relationship, able to clearly see and follow Him.

The sixth foundation stone is a PURE HEART that is continuously cleansed through repentance. This sixth mile marker is indeed the path of dominion; moreover, you simply cannot get there without it.

7) "Blessed are the peacemakers. . . ."

In the world system we live in, strife is the norm. It is seen everywhere in the world, and no one and no place is immune. In the United States, almost half of all marriages end in divorce. In the city of Chicago, more than five hundred people a year have been murdered for the last three years. Wars and military conflicts are constantly being waged, with occasional outbreaks of "nervous calm;" however, that is not for a lack of peace activists fighting to ban nuclear weapons and all wars. No. The World . . . Simply . . . Lacks . . . Peace.

In Isaiah 9:6, a prophecy is recorded concerning the earthly reign of Yeshua as the Prince of Peace. He was prophesied to rule a universal empire and end all wars. The absence of war, however, is not the only definition of peace. Peace originally existed in the garden after creation, and the first couple walked with God in a continual state of calm, secure in God's care for them. This peace is a part of God's character—who He is—and it is wrapped intrinsically into Messiah's prophetic identity. This is not something that kingdom people create but is something they carry. The more we walk in God's presence with Him, the more of His peace we experience and carry, and the more we will be identified with Him.

The seventh foundation stone is being a PEACEMAKER, that is one who knows and carries God's peace through a life lived out in His Presence. This seventh mile marker of peace identifies who the sons are. They are those who spend time in the presence of the Father.

8) "Blessed are they which are persecuted for righteousness sake. . . ."

Ever since Nimrod established a one-world government at Babel on the plain of Shinar, men have attempted to control the actions, and even the thoughts, of other men.

224 THE ENEMY OF KINGS | LOUIS EVANS

In Daniel 3, for example, after building a 90-foot gold statue of himself, Nebuchadnezzar required everyone to worship it. Not everyone agreed to go along with that idea, and the "thought police" were notified. These controlling types have existed all throughout human history (Remember the Inquisition?), and they continue to this day. If you don't believe me, just try speaking the truth of the Bible in academia or the media, and there is a good chance you will be labeled a "homophobe," "transphobe," "Islamophobe," "bigot," or the dreaded "racist." In any case, the thought police told Nebuchadnezzar about three audacious teenagers' refusals to prostrate themselves and worship that statue. Well, the king's enormous ego must have been bruised because the resulting temper tantrum caused him to order the "execution furnace" to be heated seven times hotter than normal. He then ordered his mightiest soldiers to tightly bind the teens with rope and throw them into the fire.

Three things happen when you are persecuted for thinking and acting in a godly manner:

1) Your persecutors will throw you into the fire, but they themselves will end up being destroyed by it.

2) Just as the fire burned off the ropes that held them, the persecution you experience will liberate you from the limitations placed on you by that same world system.

3) After the boys were thrown into the furnace, Nebuchadnezzar noticed a fourth person walking around in the fire that had the appearance of a "Son of God." Now, as then, the fire of persecution always attracts the presence of God.

At the end of the story, the three Hebrew boys walked out of that furnace into Nebuchadnezzar's presence; they were free, undisturbed, and without even the smell of smoke on them.

The eighth foundation stone is a willingness to ENDURE PERSECUTION for doing the right thing. This eighth mile marker of dominion reveals that those who walk in dominion are not immune from conflict with the world system and the accompanying persecution.

"Blessed are ye, when men shall revile you, and persecute you,
and say all manner of evil against you falsely, for my sake. . . ."

The eighth and ninth beatitudes, on their face, appear to be similar; however, when carefully examined, they are very different.

First, the people mentioned in the first eight beatitudes are referred to as "the" or "they." The ninth is the first time He referred to them as "ye" and "you." The focus of the world's rejection will shift from your thoughts and ideas to your "personhood."

People will revile and reject you. Then, they will say and write things about you that are deliberately and patently false in order to defame and slander your reputation. None of what they write or say is the truth but lies designed to create a false narrative about you. The rejection is not merely leveled against the individual but rather against Whom it is they serve. They are only proxies for their King.

In Matthew 5:12, Yeshua continued:

Rejoice and be exceeding glad: for great is your reward in heaven:
for so persecuted they the prophets which were before you.
The persecution of Yeshua's followers is not merely a result of what
they believe but Whom they believe and trust in and follow. It is
Messiah they truly persecute because He is not simply a religious

leader but a King! The kingdom He rules on earth stands directly opposed to the world system created by Nimrod. The world doesn't hate us because we are religious; the world hates us because they see us as squatters—on territory they consider to be their own. Therefore, we are their enemy and must be removed. The ninth and final foundation stone of Messiah's kingdom culture is a willingness to SHARE HIS SUFFERING. This final mile marker reveals that the more the dominion of the last Adam is expressed and manifested in our lives, the more opposition manifested in personal rejection we will receive.

Kingdom culture is expressed the same way Messiah lived on the earth. It is by a life lived in dominion over sin, the forces of darkness, and the damage they cause. We cannot walk in power over these things without it as nothing else has the power and authority to deliver the people of this earth from these things and accomplish the mandate God has given to us.

Kingdom culture is expressed the same way Messiah lived on the earth. It is by a life lived in dominion over sin, the forces of darkness, and the damage they cause.

CHAPTER 20

THE GLORIOUS KING

And I turned to see the voice that spake with me. And being turned,

I saw seven golden candlesticks. And in the midst of the seven

candlesticks one like unto the Son of man, clothed with a garment

down to the foot, and girt about the paps with a golden girdle. His

head and his hairs were white like wool, as white as snow; and his

eyes were as a flame of fire. And his feet were like unto fine brass, as

if burned in a furnace; and his voice as the sound of many waters.

And he had in his right hand seven stars: and out of his mouth went

a sharp two-edged sword: and his countenance as the sun shineth

in his strength, and when I saw him, I fell at his feet as dead.

—REVELATION 1:12-17

When Messiah appeared upon the earth to mankind, He came with the mandate of Isaiah 61:1 to bring:

» Emotional wholeness.

» Freedom from sin.

» Deliverance from demonic bondage.

After accomplishing this, He, according to Isaiah 53, gave His own life by suffering and dying as the ultimate atonement for the sins of mankind. This was accomplished not only to prepare their hearts for a life in the kingdom but even more so to experience intimacy with the King!

The Messianic prophecy of Isaiah 9 concerning the coming King was unveiled to John the apostle on the island of Patmos by *Yeshua* Himself. While John was exiled on this island by the Romans, as the last of the original twelve disciples still alive, he witnessed his Master's appearance from the heavenly realm. His purpose for appearing was to show John (and the rest of us), that He was no longer the Suffering Servant of Isaiah 53 that John had watched die, resurrect, and then ascend into heaven. Instead, He was now the warrior-King described in Isaiah 9 destined to conquer the entire planet and bring peace to it again.

One Sunday, while communing with God "in the Spirit," he heard an unnaturally loud voice behind him; someone, he realized, was talking to him. When he turned behind him to look, he was so amazed he did a "double take." When he turned to look the second time, he saw seven candlesticks or light stands. Now, remember, what John saw was not of this earth, so his description of what he saw is based on his own point of reference. So far, we know John heard a very loud voice and identified seven light stands of a heavenly origin. The voice identified itself as "Alpha and Omega, the first and the last," and then commanded him to record what he saw and send it to the seven churches in Asia Minor (modern-day Turkey).

Throughout the centuries, there have been many depictions of *Yeshua*. He has been portrayed as a European by some and as African by others, but most have portrayed Him as a pathetically feminine weakling. However, the reality was that He was a carpenter, which would mean he had a muscular body and an astute business mind. What John saw next would obliterate every artistic or cultural concept we have of Him.

There among the light stands John gazed upon, he also recognized someone who looked like a man but was vastly different than any human figure John had ever seen. He apparently wore a linen garment and breastplate of pure gold like a priest. He had the physicality of a warrior and the demeanor of a King. When John turned his attention to this "Son of man," he noticed a bright white light emanating from every exposed part of His body, including His head and face. In describing His head and hair, John used the similes of wool and snow: "His head and his hairs were white like wool, as white as snow." The wool describes the shine of a lamb's wool when reflecting light, and the snow describes the effervescent appearance of light reflecting from snow as it falls from the sky.

John then noticed that His eyes were wide as if staring at something remarkable. Of course, this should not come as a surprise to any of us since John was the disciple that *Yeshua* "loved." This was His favorite, and He must have been overjoyed to see him again! His eyes had the appearance of tiny flashes of lightning with a shimmering glow, and His voice sounded like the roar of a torrential downpour of rain. His right hand held seven stars. Now, the right hand signifies power, force, and means, and the seven stars, according to theologians, represent the leaders of the seven churches of Asia Minor. So, this represents His authority over the churches He was about to address. In Hebrews 4:12, we read the words:

For the word of God is quick and powerful, and sharper
than any two-edged sword, piercing even to the dividing
asunder of soul and spirit, and of joints and marrow, and is
a discerner of the thoughts and intentions of the heart.

The "word of God" in Hebrews was compared to a Roman weapon of war. It was a short sword with two very sharp edges that would slice you going in and coming out. God's Word is described as such for its ability to know what finds its origin in God, in your flesh, in your soul, or in your spirit. It is not revealed what *Yeshua* said to John using such a vivid metaphor, but it revealed deep and hidden things. Finally, John focused on His face which absolutely radiated power and loving joy, and while looking upon His face, John all at once recognized his Master. When he did, He was overcome with shock and lost consciousness.

» What John saw was not from this dimension but from a heavenly place.

» He was describing something he had never seen nor heard before.

» His voice was compared to the sound of the roar of a torrential downpour or a rushing river at flood stage.

» It was both remarkable and unearthly.

He wore a garment of a material that had the appearance of linen of a heavenly origin. It covered everything except His head, hands, and feet. He also wore a gold breastplate (described as a "band") over well-developed pectoral muscles. A brilliant white light emanated from every part of His body not covered by the linen garment or the gold breastplate. Though His face shone as bright as the sun, John was still able to describe His eyes. They were animated and excited to see His favorite disciple again. They had the appearance of flashing lightning with a heavenly glow.

> Because He fulfilled every one of God's requirements and had been completely obedient to the Father, Yeshua now had all power and authority.

Finally, because He fulfilled every one of God's requirements and had been completely obedient to the Father, *Yeshua* now had all power and authority. He wore no crown or any symbol of authority as He now possessed all authority and all power. *Yeshua's* purpose for this vision was first to reveal Himself to John and then to the church, that He was no longer the Suffering Servant of Isaiah 53. Instead, He would forever be the Isaiah 9 King of the coming universal empire.

> *And so, it is written, the first Adam was made a living*
> *soul; the last Adam was made a quickening spirit.*
> —1 CORINTHIANS 15:45

In Luke 4:18-20, *Yeshua* recited Isaiah 61:1-2 in the synagogue and then made a startling claim, that He was the fulfillment of that prophetic declaration. Now, of course, these were people who had watched Him grow up since He was a small child. They simply could not bring themselves to believe His extraordinary claim. In fact, they were deeply offended and desired to bring Him down to their level. "Isn't this Joseph's son?" they asked sarcastically. *Yeshua* then began to intentionally provoke them with reminders of times in their history when God showed favor to the gentiles over them. This aroused their passions and the demonic forces that controlled them to demonstrate the dominion of the last Adam.

Every man in the synagogue who heard and understood what *Yeshua* said was filled with "wrath" or *thymos* which is Greek for an "out of control rage." At that moment, a demonic force took control of the people, and they grabbed *Yeshua* and attempted to throw Him off of a cliff head first to His death. However, in a powerful demonstration of dominion, *Yeshua* took authority over these dark forces. With the evil spirits bound and unable to energize the people, *Yeshua* simply walked through the midst of them and went on His way. *Yeshua* never exercised dominion over people—only over the forces of darkness in people. In this case, he dealt with the demonic forces and simply walked away from those who sought to harm Him.

Yeshua taught in the synagogues all over Galilee, and He proclaimed the arrival of a new kingdom or realm. It was a time of great excitement for all the common people as He taught like He knew what He was talking about, unlike their religious leaders. The kingdom originally prophesied of in Isaiah 9 was given to Him to rule. However, the desire of the Father was for the inhabitants of *Yeshua*'s kingdom to be free and live in peace with Him. His mandate upon the earth according to Isaiah 61 was to cleanse sin, heal emotions, and deliver Adam's descendants from demons; everything else He did was accomplished with this in mind. It was observed that He healed all manner of disease, infirmity (or sickness), and debility. He healed infectious diseases like leprosy and tuberculosis and degenerative conditions like heart disease and arthritis.

From Galilee, the knowledge of Him spread as far away as Syria, and the gentiles there brought to Him those who were incurably ill, drug-addicted, trapped in depression, and mentally tormented. They also brought those who were paralyzed, demonized, or insane, and He healed them.

As the last Adam, *Yeshua,* while on the earth, exercised dominion over Lucifer, every principality, power, and ruler in the atmosphere, and every demon on the earth. Possessing that same dominion over sin, He forgave people and restored them from the curse of sin.

When God created the first Adam, he was generated to be a living soul. That is, he was created as a physical body, and then God breathed into him the *ruwach* or "breath" of God. All descendants of the first Adam (that being ALL of us) have a soul, but the last Adam is a life-giving spirit (or breath). In John 20:22, *Yeshua,* in His resurrected body, blew on His disciples and said, "Receive ye the Holy Ghost." Now, for the first time in history, the sons of Adam possessed the life of God. These "descendants" of the last Adam, from that point, possessed the capacity to give God's life that they had received to others.

What does this mean for us? In John 14:12, *Yeshua* made a remarkable declaration to His disciples:

> *Verily, verily, I say unto you, He that believeth on me, the*
> *works that I do shall he do also; and greater works than*
> *these shall he do; because I go unto my Father.*

"He that believeth" is a universal statement that refers to anyone who trusts in Yeshua's completed sacrifice for their required atonement. Once someone puts their utter trust in His completed sacrifice and repents of their rebellion against God, He promised that all the works He did upon the earth, His disciples would do also. The reason He said that our works would be greater is because when Yeshua left the earth, He promised to send the Holy Ghost to invade the lives of His followers. This would allow Him to multiply His capabilities all over the earth. Therefore, just as Yeshua is a life-giving spirit, so will God's Spirit duplicate that capability in every one of His followers.

In the world of design engineering, a team of engineers may be tasked to design a widget (a car, appliance, aircraft, etc.). The item is then thoroughly described in a document called a "drawing." The engineering drawing documents every requirement it must possess to perform its function completely. It will even describe how long each component must last. Then that team of engineers will use the drawing to build the first widget called a "prototype." After this first article is built, it is vigorously and even brutally tested. When the testing has been completed, production can begin because the engineers are confident the design will do what it was designed to do. It does not matter how many are produced, each widget can be trusted to successfully perform its function.

Though *Yeshua* was declared the very Son of God, being fully God and fully man, God very carefully described every aspect of His coming, His mandate, and His assignment—He would die, and He would rise again and rule for eternity. As the prototype of a new race, *Yeshua* was tested in the wilderness with hunger and lack. He was tempted to act independently of God, to desire the Nimrod system, and to sin sexually—yes, sexually, but He never sinned! During His earthly ministry, He brought freedom from sin, healing of body and soul, and deliverance from demonic bondage and torment. He rebuked the wind and waves, supernaturally fed thousands of people, and even raised the dead back to life. Did the prototype testing stop there? Not on your life! He was betrayed by someone that He lived, ate, and traveled with for three years, and it didn't make Him bitter. He was savagely beaten in the face by men's fists, then whipped until his flesh hung from his body, and His organs were exposed. Then He was nailed to a cross with nine-inch iron spikes. Yet even in the midst of all His suffering, He forgave His tormentors.

> The forces of darkness and the world system assaulted Him relentlessly, yet the design still held!

When He was buried in a tomb, He refused to stay there and raised Himself three days later. Why is this so important? According to Scripture, *Yeshua* is the "first born of many brethren," which means if you have given your life to Him and you have received the gift of His blood as an atonement for your sin, then you are a copy of the prototype. Everything—yes, everything—that's true of the prototype is true of each copy. The life that *Yeshua* lived proved the Scriptures though all the forces of darkness were arrayed against Him. The forces of darkness and the world system assaulted Him relentlessly, yet the design still held!

What does this mean for us? It means that *Yeshua's* life is the standard against which every human life will be measured. He proved that a man can live a life free from sin. I'm not referring to "sinless perfection" but a life lived in perfect intimacy, a life lived in such intimacy with the Father that His presence will constrain you and make sin so disgusting that you unequivocally flee it.

It means that *Yeshua's* mandate from Isaiah 61:1-2 is to prepare His people for the kingdom He will rule according to the prophecy of Isaiah 9. He did this in three ways:

1) *He imparted His eternal truths using temporal principles.*
2) He can empower us to teach others not only to live in the absence of sin but in the presence of righteousness.

   He imparted this divine life through a heart of compassion.
3) We can learn and teach others to bring healing to the souls and bodies of others.

   He imparted His divine authority.
4) We can be instrumental in the deliverance of others from the forces of darkness.

Yeshua walked in authority over His environment and carried this boldness everywhere He went. He possessed a sober and judicious temperament but walked fearlessly. In fact, when His disciples thought they were going to die during a storm, *Yeshua* simply commanded the storm to be quiet, and when it calmed down, He just went back to sleep. With this legacy, we can live in the same courage and peace.

Yeshua also walked in perfect wisdom, able to perfectly navigate a corrupt religious system and a world political system devoid of any kind of Godly influence. He also possessed a perfect knowledge of the Law and the Prophets that was unsurpassed then or at any time since. Yet, it was not He who would evangelize the world, but millions of copies endowed with the power and authority of the Holy Ghost would do it.

Yeshua, ultimately, suffered mental, emotional, and physical anguish at the hands of the people He came to save, yet most of them rejected Him. From the death of Stephen in the Book of Acts up to today, untold numbers of believers have suffered prison, privation, and pain for the sake of the gospel, and many have even given their lives. It was *Yeshua* who proved that it was possible for the believer to carry his or her cross and die upon it if called to do so.

EPILOGUE

About seven years after my marriage to Chandra in late 2012, I started the writing of this book based on my devotional study of the Book of Proverbs. I can say with all confidence that this has probably been the most difficult undertaking of my life. I even quit writing for several months, having told myself that I couldn't do it, until Pastor Tony Foster prophetically rebuked me for my disobedience. I know with great certainty that Satan is not at all happy with the content of this book and has contended with me every step of the way. But for the grace of God, I would never have been able to finish this project. Nevertheless, God, in His faithfulness, has continued to provide the grace for me to continue, and here we are at the end. I am going to wrap this up with a few more thoughts, and then we'll be done.

In the first section, I spoke at length about dominion. This is a word that is misused a great deal today. *Elohim* endued the first man and woman with unique capabilities and the authority to fulfill His mandate for them at that time. This was to rule the earth, produce copies of themselves by childbearing, and bring judgment upon the forces of darkness by treading on them. When the first couple rebelled, they lost that authority and mandate, but God gave them the promise of redemption in a future Messiah who would succeed where they had failed.

When *Yeshua* came, He exercised dominion as Adam would have. However, with this first trip to earth, *Yeshua* was primarily preoccupied with reproducing Himself on the earth by teaching and empowering twelve men with the Holy Spirit. When *Yeshua* left the earth to return to the Father, He sent the Holy Spirit to empower them to produce the "greater works." Their (what I call) "Dominion Mandate" was the same as *Yeshua's* mandate towards the people He ministered to. According to Isaiah 61:1-2, this included:

1) Setting people free from the drive to sin so that they can walk in purity and righteousness before God. This way they would be able to pursue relationship with Him freely instead of hiding from Him in fear.

2) Healing their damaged emotions to allow them to enter into relationships without damaging those around them. This, in turn, would promote successful relationships like marriage and child-rearing and act as a check upon family dysfunction. It would also strengthen the body of Christ, allowing its members to sharpen one another without devouring each other.

3) Setting them free from the forces of darkness, releasing them from the control and/or influence of vile spirit life-forms that desire to destroy them. This could be as simple as the fever Yeshua rebuked from disturbing Peter's mother-in-law in Luke 4:38-40 to the Gadarene man He delivered who had been inhabited by a whole legion of demons (approximately six thousand) in Mark 5.

4) Though *Yeshua* performed a great number of miracles, signs, and wonders, His highest priority for His people is still this three-part mandate, and anytime the miraculous receives more attention than *Yeshua's* mandate, it is out of balance.

I dedicated section two to talking about wisdom and its application in daily life. Please understand that even though much of what I discussed hinges on the involvement of your parents in your life, not having involved parents (especially a present father) doesn't disqualify you from receiving God's wisdom and understanding. The way to receive God's wisdom is to ask for it, be willing to listen to the voices of the people who have suffered through tough lessons of life, and, finally, be teachable. The most practical issues of life deal with money and sex—their use and misuse. In their proper context, they are a joy to have and experience, but when abused, they are the source of great misery. The world system controls the information and will not tell you this. Hollywood won't. Media won't. Academia definitely won't. The only source of true wisdom is from God as revealed in the Bible, especially the Book of Proverbs. Books like this one are often helpful, but there is no substitute for God's words expressed in the Bible.

Though Yeshua performed a great number of miracles, signs, and wonders, His highest priority for His people is still this three-part mandate, and anytime the miraculous receives more attention than Yeshua's mandate, it is out of balance.

Finally, in section three I spoke about the world system and the tension between living in it and yet not belonging to it. *Yeshua* proved that it was possible to do both as He was born and raised in a country under Roman occupation. This was during a period in Jewish history where even the high priests were a part of the world system having been appointed by the Roman government. The religious leaders had sold out their convictions and found *Yeshua* to be a threat to their influence and power. During a confrontation with the Herodians' and the Pharisees' disciples, He was asked, "Is it lawful to give tribute unto Caesar or not?" This was not prompted by a desire for spiritual insight. It was a question meant to trap Him. If He replied and said it was not lawful, he could be arrested by the Romans and accused of treason. If He said it was lawful, He would be called a "sell-out" and considered a traitor to His people by aligning Himself with a foreign occupier. To this intended trap question, Jesus brilliantly responded, "Render therefore unto Caesar the things which are Caesar's; and unto God the things which are God's" (Matthew 22:21). The reason He asked for a coin was to point out that what Caesar wanted was external. He wanted their money (taxes) and for their civil laws to be obeyed. God wanted their hearts. He also wanted their willing obedience. That should be our relationship with the world today—to be righteous, obedient citizens that live righteous, peaceful lives and pray for those in authority over us. While we do not belong to the world system, neither do we adhere in any way to its culture. We adhere to the culture of God's kingdom.

As the *protos* of Revelation 22:13, *Yeshua* is the "First," the prototype of a new race. Everything that He did on the earth, we can do also, especially live holy lives—not simply free of the obvious sins like fornication and drunkenness but also the hidden sins like pride and bitterness. It was the late Leonard Ravenhill that once said, "The greatest miracle that God can do today is to take an unholy man out of an unholy world and make him holy, then put him back into that unholy world and keep him holy in it."

Yeshua also came to heal our emotions because the fall has damaged all of us. Every one of us is damaged by the sin of our ancestors, our own sins, and sins perpetrated against us. We are all in need of walking through the process of sanctification. This can often be facilitated by any program or method that that helps you to walk through introspection, asking God to search your heart (Psalm 139:23-24):

> *Search me, O God, and know my heart: try me, and*
> *know my thoughts: And see if there be any wicked way*
> *in me, and lead me in the way everlasting.*

You cannot walk in sustained dominion authority, carrying out *Yeshua's* mandate, without this process of sanctification carried out and continuing in your life. There are many programs, but I highly recommend:

> *Healing the Heart*
>
> *Living Waters Ministry*
>
> *www.livingwatersministry.com*

In any case, my desire is for God to richly transform your life through the contents of this book. Its purpose is to transform your life and increase it, so you can be fruitful, multiply, and exercise dominion over the enemy of kings. In the name of *Yeshua,* our King!